Transformational EMDR

THE MANUAL

SHAPIRO'S ASPIRATION FOR EMDR BEYOND THE DISEASE MODEL

Dr. Andrew J. Dobo

with

M.H. Johnson • Elena Engle • Carolyn Lenz
Robert Engle • Linda Khmelnytska
Ryan Terry • Dunja Pacirski

Soul Psych Publishers
Melbourne, Florida

Transformational EMDR: The Manual
Shapiro's Aspiration for EMDR Beyond the Disease Model

Published by
Soul Psych Publishers
1270 North Wickham Road
Suite 16-602
Melbourne, Florida

Cover Design: Sky Diary Productions

Paperback ISBN: 978-0-9962207-8-1

Library of Congress Cataloging-in-publication Data Pending

Contents

Introduction

Five or ten years ago, there would have been no need for this book. My experience with EMDR at the time, along with my small community of EMDR clinicians, was that we were practicing EMDR as taught, which aligned with Francine Shapiro's teachings. Today, many clinicians claim to use EMDR as a model, but what they are doing often seems unrecognizable to me. Someone asked me recently if I use the water glasses when I do EMDR. I did not even want to ask, what on earth is water glass EMDR? I said no, did not ask for an explanation, and left it at that.

This book has a twofold purpose. First, this book will identify elements that have been added to Shapiro's model, which are almost considered staples of EMDR today, that tragically dilute EMDR's power at best or completely render it useless or even harmful to clients at worst.

Poorly trained EMDR clinicians are often terrified of what might happen when they administer EMDR, so they spend months preparing and resourcing, not because the client needs all of this resourcing, but because the clinicians are afraid of the emotional discharge EMDR might cause. Shapiro warned about the therapist's lack of tolerance for high emotion as a serious problem back in 2003. We will cover every limiting and damaging addition to the EMDR model and provide its antidote that comes primarily from Shapiro's own words.

Secondly, we introduce EMDR as a robust process to accelerate individuation and transformation, using it from the non-disease model as a self-actualizing accelerant that Shapiro mentioned. For this non-disease method to be understood and utilized, the EMDR clinician must know that EMDR is a psychoanalytic process (Leeds, 2016); its use reaches beyond symptom resolution. Shapiro aspired to have EMDR used as a method for self-actualization, which Jung would call individuation—becoming who we are meant to be. This book teaches EMDR clinicians exactly how to conceptualize cases from this perspective and how to use EMDR to transform their clients' lives, beyond eliminating symptoms.

Shapiro discusses self-actualization only twice, and she does not specify how to achieve it. It has been my life's work to figure this out, and I have done so. This book is a road map, a blueprint for therapists who wish to use EMDR to transform their clients' lives, guiding them to their authentic purpose and true self, free and unencumbered by their past. This book takes over where Shapiro's self-actualizing aspiration left off.

We take our marching orders from Shapiro's words, literally. Francine laid out how to administer EMDR from the adaptive information processing model clearly and concisely in her 2001, second edition of *Eye Movement Desensitization and Reprocessing* (EMDR) *Therapy: Basic Principles, Protocols, and Procedures*, and again in 2018 in the third edition. She also gave several keynote addresses around the time of the second book, in which she described how to administer EMDR from the AIP model. This book uses the 2003 keynote address at the EMDRIA conference in Denver, titled *The Adaptive Information Processing Model and Case Conceptualization*, as its primary reference. It compares how Shapiro instructs EMDR therapists to administer EMDR versus how it is being administered now in 2025.

In this comparison, we hope to return EMDR to a healthy future by reminding everyone of its past. One might call this effort, as the kids say, "EMDR the O.G." We also use EMDR as a self-actualizing accelerant, again taking Shapiro's lead when she said, "Not just [self-]actualization for some. [Self-]actualization for everyone" (Shapiro, 2003). With this, we describe how to use EMDR from a non-disease model toward self-actualization and individuation—again, using Shapiro's own words as our motivation to heal all clients, not just those who meet an insurance-driven mental health diagnosis.

Prologue

Those of you who know me are aware that I am an EMDR-trained therapist with a Jungian background. Although this is an EMDR book, it is only right to start with a quote by C.G. Jung: "If you do your work truly and conscientiously, unknown allies will come and seek you out."

I am an introvert by nature and have worked quietly for most of my life. I strive to be true and conscientious in my work. More recently, I have had a more public presence—not anything I cherish, but I feel at this stage of my life, it is my purpose. Over the past seven years, I have trained over a thousand therapists in the proper administration of EMDR, and a handful of these trainees have been drawn to my work. These are my allies, the allies Jung guaranteed would seek me out. He was right. Initially, some of these allies were skeptical about this weird EMDR thing, but they all soon were surprised by its incredible healing power when done correctly.

These six allies are the "friends" mentioned on the cover

of this book, whom you will meet in this book. I asked each of them to write a chapter, a chapter that suits their experience and skill set. It is a pleasure working with these six dedicated clinicians, who have coined the term "Transformational EMDR™" to differentiate it from what we typically think of as EMDR, a mental health treatment. I believe it was Ryan Terry, LMHC, who first distinguished between regular symptom resolution EMDR, which we all do, versus the Transformational EMDR approach that I have developed, practiced, and written about. Ryan's description led to the development of a formalization of this approach. This, in turn, led to Transformational EMDR certification and the writing of this book to guide clinicians in the self-actualizing use of EMDR. This certification allows us to distinguish between those who work in this in-depth manner and those who do not. If you are reading this book, we hope you will join us in bringing clients to their authentic selves and true purpose.

It has been and continues to be a privilege working with this small group of skilled and dedicated clinicians. Here in my seventieth year, they energize me. They make me excited to go to work with them. Hopefully, they gain wisdom from my years of experience. It is a rich exchange between mentor and mentees that makes us all better EMDR clinicians, teachers, and hopefully, better people. It keeps us all passionate and excited about the work. We often email each other, "I have to tell you what happened in a session today. It was incredible." Or, "I have to tell you about a dream I had last night to see what you think."

So I hope you will take the time to metabolize this book. I

hope you will stop adding to EMDR unnecessarily. I hope this book will encourage you to consider becoming a Transformational EMDR (T-EMDR) therapist, as Shapiro has asked us all to be when she said, "[self-]actualization for everyone." I hope you will discover your own negative cognition if you have not done so, and seek out a transformational EMDR therapist to assist you in moving through your six stages of transformation. Like the saying goes, "You can't shrink until you have been shrunk."

This is your invitation. The first step of transformation is avoidance. If you resist this invitation or postpone it, welcome to the journey, because you are in stage one.

Chapter 1

What Is Transformational EMDR?

History, Discovery, and Development

Dr. Andrew J. Dobo

I was first trained in EMDR in 1998 while earning my doctoral degree at Florida Tech. This was only three years after Shapiro's first text, *Eye Movement Desensitization and Reprocessing (EMDR) Therapy: Basic Principles, Protocols, and Procedures*, was released (1995). When EMDR came onto the scene in the early '90s, every mental health professional already had a model of therapy they were using to treat their patients. At this time, clinicians had to figure out how to integrate EMDR into their existing treatment approaches.

The mental health world was not sure what to do with this unusual therapy, where there is little talking and, in that silence, the client is asked to move their eyes back and forth while thinking of an upsetting memory. Surprisingly, almost without exception, the disturbing memories vanished. The early research confirmed these extraordinary results, initially with victims of trauma. The early research studies caused EMDR—Eye Movement Desensitization and Reprocessing—to be the recommended procedure for treating trauma.

In Shapiro's first book, EMDR was considered a procedure. It was a tool for the proverbial therapist's toolbox. After witnessing and consulting on hundreds of EMDR sessions, Shapiro noticed that EMDR had a broader range of applications. Something more important than simply desensitizing an image or memory was happening. Six years after the first book was published, Shapiro published the second edition of *Basic Principles, Protocols, and Procedures.* This book expanded the use of EMDR beyond a procedure to use for trauma. In the second book, Shapiro presents EMDR as a comprehensive model of psychotherapy. EMDR evolved into a standalone model known as the Adaptive Information Processing Model (AIPM). In this new iteration of EMDR, there was no need to integrate EMDR with other models. EMDR was understood to be a model unto itself. It was no longer a tool for the proverbial toolbox. It was the toolbox.

In my early training (1998), I used EMDR as a procedure, not as a model. I used it for trauma; that was it. I was unsure how to utilize EMDR in this more expansive manner. Fortunately, I had a few things working in my favor to understand this expanded use of EMDR. I had an excellent EMDR trainer and consultant, William Zangwill, PhD, who had been using EMDR as a model long before the second book was published.

Secondly, I was able to purchase a CD of Francine Shapiro's 2003 EMDRIA keynote address at the EMDRIA conference titled *The Adaptive Informational Processing Model (AIPM) and Case Conceptualization*, in which she clearly and concisely explains how to administer EMDR as a model. I consumed the new book and listened to that CD on my way to work and back for at least a year. I would listen and then treat patients with EMDR from this new perspective. This CD was my guide. I listened to every word Francine spoke until I had that talk practically memorized. I administered the AIPM model as she instructed, and I still do.

This speech provided incredible protection from unnecessary tampering with the model that is a plague across the EMDR landscape today. This book presents EMDR as Shapiro always intended EMDR to be practiced.

This book should not be necessary, but it is. It is Shapiro's method that has somehow been lost in these altered forms of bilateral stimulation, which are often masked as EMDR. It is like the telephone game, where you say a message to a person and the message is whispered around the room. By the time it reaches the last person, it has lost all connection to the original message. So it is with EMDR. It is unrecognizable, and this book is an attempt to return to the first message whispered in our ear.

Shapiro mentions in her book and briefly in her 2003 talk that EMDR can be used to help people achieve self-actualization. This self-actualization approach to EMDR is grounded in a non-disease model perspective. Regrettably, or fortunately for me, she mentions it briefly but never expands or explains precisely how to use EMDR in this manner. Few people, if anyone, noticed this idea. But I did. This self-actualizing statement of hers hit me like a lightning bolt. I was a student of Jungian psychology my entire life. I picked up my first Jung book in 1976 and began my journey with Jung in my twenties. Shapiro's self-actualization is what Jung referred to as the process of individuation. During those few moments when Shapiro mentioned self-actualization, I was listening! These statements invited me to value what has been my personal journey and bring it into my life's work, which is EMDR.

I am aware of only a few occasions where Shapiro mentions EMDR to be used from a non-disease-model perspective.

> They (our clients) deserve all the attributes that Maslow (1970) describes as self-actualization. To that end, we use a standard three-pronged EMDR therapy protocol to afford all clients a comprehensive treatment of past, present, and future (Shapiro, 1995, 2001, 2018).

Then again, in her speech.

> You know it's [the non-disease model use of EMDR] like not just actualization for some. [It's] actualization for everyone, into positive; it's not a disease model. We just don't want them to be limping along; we want them to be dancing (Shapiro, 2003).

My career has evolved in a way that enables me to explain precisely how to utilize EMDR as a self-actualizing and individuating tool for this transformational process. It is the use of EMDR from a non-disease model, as Shapiro mentioned, that completely transforms people's lives.

My first two books look at this transformational journey as a six-stage process. The first book presents the scientific perspective on these six stages and highlights parallels with Western religions. The second book examines the six stages and identifies the twelve steps of the mythic hero Joseph Campbell writes about that are present within these stages. The point of these comparisons is that self-actualization and individuation are universal human experiences that transcend cultural and temporal boundaries. These stages are inherent to the human experience, and EMDR accelerates the process. This book is dedicated to teaching others how to administer EMDR in this life-transforming way that is beyond symptom resolution.

As we proceed, you will gain an understanding of the discovery, stages, and application of the AIP model to facilitate transformative change in your clients' lives. The use of EMDR in this manner is known as Transformational EMDR, a method I developed and now teach.

Throughout this book, I will share Shapiro's words and then explain their relevance to Transformational EMDR. Her words were and continue to be the catalyst for Transformational EMDR. Here are the words that started this journey for me.

> Someone comes in with a driving phobia. If I just concentrate on the driving phobia and send her back to a life of quiet desperation, I wouldn't personally consider that good work unless that's all she's willing to do, but as a clinician, if I'm taking a history and seeing the larger clinical picture, at least let me make the person aware of the possibilities and the potential to see if there's other things, because a symptom like a phobia or PTSD can

> simply be masking. It's like taking the quilt off the mattress. You know there can be a lot of lumps and bumps that you need to deal with, so if I take a good clinical history, I'm able to identify what might need to be processed to help get this person to an *actualized state* (Shapiro, 2003).

This quote permitted me to think about Jung, individuation, and EMDR. Jungian thought influenced my early interest in psychology and self-growth. Individuation was a term I was familiar with, as I diligently worked on myself to move forward in my life through journaling, engaging in dream work, and discussing these topics with a small community of Jungian friends and mentors who were also on the same journey.

This inner journey all started when I was an undergraduate studying music in Chicago. I was not familiar with much else in the world of psychology beyond Jungian dream work. My focus was music back then. I journaled for decades and still do. I think that, due to my internal journey, this self-actualizing statement stuck in my mind, even though Shapiro only referenced it once in her book and once in her speech; it resonated with me. Most other clinicians focused on different elements of EMDR. For me, this self-actualizing suggestion opened a door that connected my personal worldview to my work as a psychologist.

Using EMDR as a non-disease model gave me permission to go beyond symptom resolution and encourage my clients to "dance out of the office" rather than dragging themselves out of the office to live a life of quiet desperation. Four life experiences influenced my work and life, helping me to develop, understand, and create Transformational EMDR.

The first was my lifelong interest in dreams, individuation, and journaling, which I just mentioned. This decades-long practice provided me with an in-depth understanding of the language of the unconscious and the individuation process. I was open to dreams and synchronistic events (meaningful coincidences), as Jung described, and I have experienced dozens of them, if not hundreds. I have witnessed numerous synchronistic events in my monthly trainings of EMDR as well. These mystical-like events happen in every training.

In my private practice, clients often brought dreams into their sessions. I was comfortable working with these dreams. Over the years, it has become clear that there are four dream themes that people move through during the Transformational EMDR process, which I discuss in detail in my second book, *The Hero's Journey: Integrating Jungian Psychology and EMDR Therapy*, and we will briefly discuss in a later chapter. The first component of inner exploration made me the ideal person to recognize the Transformational EMDR patterns that appeared in their dreams. This skill helped me identify the four dream themes that are consistent and predictable in this six-stage process.

The second element was a specific dream a client brought to me. This client was symptom-free after a year of intense trauma work. I discharged her from treatment, but after six months, she returned to therapy angry with me, saying, "What did you do to me?"

"When I had PTSD, at least I knew why I was anxious

and upset. Now I do not have any anxiety or symptoms, but I am miserable."

She also shared a dream that she did not understand. This dream made her angry. She was not religious because her abuser was a highly respected man in the church. She wanted nothing to do with God or religion. Her dream had religious elements. In a way, that dream was for me; I understood it. This dream began to solidify the stages of transformation. This dream was a loss of identity dream, a dream about confusion. I recall reading what Jung said about chaos and confusion: "All psychological transformation requires a period of chaos and confusion." Shapiro warns us about this stage. She described it as the client's experience of a loss of identity.

This dream was about St. Elizabeth, the mother of John the Baptist. The Blessed Virgin Mary visited St. Elizabeth when she was pregnant with Jesus. This dream represented the stage preceding the birth of the Savior, the birth of new life for my client. She was metaphorically in labor, waiting for the new way to emerge. Once I understood that, we set out to self-actualize and individuate, making a solid shift from the old way to a new life. This dream was the first time I experienced a loss of identity with a client after successful treatment. Then the Jungian quote of transformation made sense because I could see it right in front of me with this client.

The final element was an experience that changed my entire perception of clients and the use of EMDR. I attended an Emotionally Focused Couples workshop to hear Sue Johnson, PhD. In this talk, she said that every couple has an *I'm not good enough* person and an *I don't matter* person in the relationship. She calls them pursuers and withdrawers. *I don't matter* people pursue, and *I'm not good enough* people withdraw. She also said that in about 15 percent of couples, you have either two *I don't matter* people or two *I'm not good enough* people in the relationship.

This statement changed my life. I was working from EMDR as a procedure perspective, not yet from a model, and certainly not a non-disease model. However, this was the final experience that helped me understand and develop the Transformational EMDR method. The two cognitions Johnson described are different than the cognitions on the list Shapiro provides in her model. In EMDR, you find the target and match it with the negative cognition, which is how the EMDR procedure works.

Hearing Sue Johnson say that everyone has one or both of these two cognitions shook up my world. These two cognitions are different. I soon realized that these two cognitions were the magic key to the kingdom that can cause cataclysmic changes in a client when used in conjunction with EMDR. These are the life experiences that brought Transformational EMDR to light.

1. Lifelong Jungian interest in dreams, individuation, and self-growth. These decades of working with dreams created a familiarity with unconscious material that many other EMDR clinicians lacked.
2. Shapiro's keynote, where she discusses self-actualizing EMDR as a non-disease model,

resonated with me as I saw EMDR shift from a procedure to a model.

3. The St. Elizabeth dream and understanding that chaos and confusion are necessary ingredients for psychological transformation.
4. These two powerful negative cognitions are common to everyone. People usually have one or sometimes both of these transformational negative cognitions.

The die was cast for me to explore the non-disease use of EMDR, which led to the development of Transformational EMDR. Transformational EMDR is the most potent use of EMDR. After reading this book, I hope you will agree.

Chapter 2

The Transformational EMDR therapist?

The Requirements and Differences

Dr. Andrew J. Dobo

Difference Number One: *We trust the psychoanalytic self-healing process that is EMDR.*

Transformational EMDR requires a deep mastery of the standard EMDR protocol. T-EMDR therapists rarely add another model to this process. The standard protocol is not tampered with in any way. Transformational EMDR uses the original eight-phase adaptive informational processing model (AIPM).

When I say mastery of the standard protocol, I do not mean a basic understanding of the EMDR rubrics but rather an understanding of every granular moment that occurs in an EMDR processing session. This detailed understanding is often not explored because current trends in EMDR therapy require integrating models with EMDR rather than having a thorough, in-depth knowledge of the material that the standard protocol provides. An understanding of psychoanalytic language is necessary because it is often the most robust material that presents itself in sessions, but few people understand the language of the psyche. Transformational EMDR therapists do.

Recently, rather than therapists understanding psychoanalytic language, the trend is that EMDR isn't working and it needs other models to complete the process of EMDR therapy. Transformational EMDR therapists rarely need to use additional models. There are times when a problem arises and creativity is required. In these cases, the more you know, the better, including other models.

This in-depth understanding of the EMDR process first recognizes that EMDR is indeed a psychoanalytic process (Leeds, 2016). Second, it is also a self-healing process (Shapiro, 1995, 2001, 2018). The Transformational EMDR therapist lives these realities. They accept that EMDR is psychoanalytic and are, therefore, trained in psychoanalytic language and processes. Not so much to include or integrate a psychoanalytic model with EMDR, but to recognize the psychoanalytic material that naturally manifests during EMDR therapy.

Few EMDR therapists are trained in psychoanalytic language; thus, they miss half of the valuable material that presents itself during EMDR. This lack of awareness is why clinicians often seek other models for help. Transformational EMDR therapists rarely miss anything. They are entirely attuned to every breath, every somatization, and statements that the client's process creates.

The Transformational EMDR therapist understands that the less they say, instruct, or help, the better. They know that what they say has little or nothing to do with the healing power of EMDR. Since 1995, and probably before that, Shapiro has said that EMDR is self-healing, imploring the therapist to simply stay out of the way.

Difference Number Two: *Transformational EMDR therapists create and maintain their client's state of flow, which we will discuss later, at all costs.*

The T-EMDR therapist trusts that the client will reach their desired destination and patiently allows the self-healing power of EMDR to be accessed and maintained without interruption. For this to happen, the therapist takes a back seat while intensely waiting, watching and listening.

Flow is described as the optimal human experience and the ultimate experience of living in the moment. Transformational EMDR therapists create the environment for accessing flow. In an ideal session, both the client and the therapist are in the state of flow simultaneously. For this to happen, the therapist must stop thinking and just wait, watch, and listen, trusting that what you need will occur in the moment it needs to be experienced.

A deep confidence to "trust the process" is essential. To allow whatever wants to happen, to happen without fear, is a requisite skill. This manner of administering EMDR requires a deep trust in the model, your inner self, your skill, and the self-healing power of the client. Just as the client must trust you, you must trust yourself and EMDR. The Transformational EMDR therapist creates an environment where the self-healing power is present. This environment occurs when thinking and preconceived ideas stop. Instead, the goal is to wait, watch, and listen. All thinking ends when the stimulation begins. Self-healing requires a state of mind that is beyond thinking. In fact, thinking prevents access to the client's self-healing ability. Transformational EMDR is not a thinking thing. Why is this so important? Your conscious mind can process forty bits of information per second, but the unconscious mind, which feeds your gut and intuition, can process 20 million bits of information per second. That is a 500,000:1 ratio, and this is why it is essential to stop thinking and just wait, watch and listen (Voss, 2025).

Difference Number Three: *The T-EMDR therapist utilizes psychoanalytic language.*

Few EMDR practitioners understand the elements of the psychoanalytic language that are commonly expressed during EMDR sessions. Most people are unaware that such a thing exists despite hearing the material every day while administering EMDR therapy.

The lack of awareness of this unconscious language's presence often causes valuable material to be squandered and lost when it appears in sessions. Material from the client's unconscious mind is the most robust and healing material that manifests during a standard EMDR session. Hopefully, this book will bring attention to this incredible material and clinicians will begin to utilize the psychoanalytic elements in their EMDR work.

This lack of knowledge causes clinicians to miss about half of the valuable material during a standard EMDR session. This failure is compounded by clinicians thinking they have to add things to the process, which further dilutes the effectiveness of EMDR. Clinicians often reach for other models because they are unaware of the most potent material that emerges organically during EMDR sessions. This is not surprising because the unconscious speaks in common, unremarkable, and overused phrases that are rarely noticed. Transformational EMDR therapists recognize that the AIP model, the standard protocol of EMDR, brings forth this powerful material, and for this reason EMDR typically does not require additional support from other models.

Difference Number Four: *Transformational EMDR is client-centered in profound ways.*

Transformational EMDR starts and ends with the client. Most EMDR therapists are aware that EMDR is a client-centered approach. We often pay lip service to the idea of following the client, but we rarely follow through with it. We have a treatment plan, goals, and agendas for our clients. We have time limits. The medical model we have come to follow has no time for following the client. Transformational EMDR therapists follow the client almost to a fault.

What do I mean by following the client? For example, in the microcosm, every set should vary in length. The set should be determined by what is going on with the client. If a therapist has a predetermined length of passes for a set, which is ridiculous on its face, that is not client-centered; that is therapist-centered.

A keenly observant transformational therapist knows that a set can range from fifteen passes to two hundred passes or more, depending on what the client needs. It depends on what the client is telling the clinician. It depends on the client's breath, their words, facial expressions, and many other factors that the therapist is attending to. During EMDR stimulation, the transformational therapist does not take notes, count passes, or time sets; the therapist should also be in a state of flow. Flow is impossible if the therapist is distracted by such meaningless tasks. T-EMDR therapists wait, watch, and listen. They have access to 20,000 bits of information per second, not forty bits per second.

In the macrocosm of the client's life, for example, the apparent material shared by the client when they walk in the door for the session is often squandered because the therapist has a plan for the day's agenda. The plan is to target your abusive father today, so when the client walks into the room and is upset because their neighbor blocked their driveway and almost made them late, well, this event is ignored. Immediately, the therapist moves to the plan. We are targeting your abusive father today. At first glance, a temporarily blocked driveway may seem unremarkable. However, in reality, it serves as a conduit for the unconscious to speak to the therapist and functions like an ally, assisting in the therapeutic process.

Shapiro warns against planning the sessions.

> Allowing processing to progress unimpeded can be extremely difficult for many clinicians (Shapiro, 2018).

Unimpeded does not only apply to EMDR stimulation. It applies to what the client brings to every session. The preconceived plan for the session usually takes precedence. The Transformational EMDR therapists know that any preconceived plan is always Plan B and the issue the client walks into the session with is Plan A. Ignoring the client's complaint about her blocked driveway is exactly what "not following the client" looks like in a session. Because our plan is usually Plan A, it is a clear example of why EMDR is not always client-centered but rather therapist-led. Most EMDR therapists' plans are sacrosanct when their plan should be "an" option, not "the" option.

Rigid thinking without clinical judgment is detrimental to the EMDR process. Shapiro reiterates:

> Clinicians must resist any preconceived notion or interference in relation to their thoughts and ideas. Their job is to allow the client to "self-heal" (Shapiro, 2018).
>
> Daniel Kahneman put it this way; Kurt Lewin's insight was if you want to achieve change in behavior there is a good way and a bad way. The good way is by diminishing restraining forces not by increasing the driving forces (Klotz, 2021).

A complaint about an event that occurred that day must be taken seriously. It should not be ignored, no matter how insignificant it may seem. Release the restraining forces of the therapist's plan and follow the driving forces the client brings into the session.

Let's examine our blocked driveway complaint to see what lies beneath. This client walks into the session, agitated and upset that someone blocked her in her driveway. You planned to address her abusive father in today's session, but she kept talking about being blocked in her driveway this morning. Why is the driveway more critical than the abusive father? What is the implicit message if someone blocks your driveway? "You do not matter" to your neighbor. The excessive agitation is telling the clinician that this seemingly less important event, when compared to an abusive father, is not less important at all.

Furthermore, if you guide her to work on her abusive father rather than listen to her distress, you are sending the same message to her as the guy who blocked her driveway. Her voice does not matter; she did not matter to the neighbor who blocked her driveway, just like she did not matter to her parents, and now she does not matter to you. You are ignoring her voice because you have a plan. You know what is best. So you continue with the abusive father target rather than following the client.

Targeting the blocked driveway evokes a negative cognition of *I don't matter*. This client, with an abusive father and mother, has the same negative cognition. We know that when the adaptive information processing model breaks down, the past is present, and this present event, which is already activating the client, will link to past childhood events. This session will have a profound healing effect by following the client.

Transformational EMDR therapists always listen to what walks in the door, no matter how unimportant it seems, because if the client tells it to you in a therapy session, it is not inconsequential. The value is not always immediately evident; this is a matter of trusting the process. Not just when stimulation is happening but anytime you are in the presence of the client, trust what is happening. Set your agenda aside and trust what walks in the door.

The therapist must also surrender to the process by allowing it to play out. Both the patient and therapist must surrender to the process. So, following the client means you listen to them. Set aside your plan and allow their life experience, internal experience, and voice to guide you in determining the next target. Do not think you know what is best because you do not. The client often does not know either, but their unconscious will reveal it if you listen.

Never "always" do anything! Every situation is unique, and the situation should determine what needs to be done, not some preconceived idea of what "I always do." For example, I always end the set after thirty passes. I also close every session with a resource.

You never do anything. You should never predetermine the set length. Everything depends on following the client. You cannot treat each client the same. If you created a cookie-cutter approach in the way you administer EMDR, you are doing a distilled version of this tremendously powerful process.

Therapists come to me for certification, and they say they always use a resource at the end of every session. This kind of rigid thinking and behavior shows that they are not following the client. We understand that processing continues even after the client leaves the office. The Transformational EMDR therapist is acutely aware of the adaptive shift to Phase Five. They also know that if the client is thinking adaptively at the end of the session, you do not want to shut that down with a resource. Unnecessary resourcing can terminate processing. Do not do that.

There are only two reasons to use a resource in a session. First, the client wants to stop while they are upset. Resourcing is required to calm the client before they leave the session. The second reason is when the client is upset and the session is coming to a close, but they are still in Phase Four and upset. Again, resourcing is used to calm the client before they leave the office. Resourcing is never done after an adaptive shift, yet well-meaning clinicians often employ a cookie-cutter approach by using a resource at the end of every session. This improper use of resourcing is another example of not following the client but imposing "the plan" or routine onto the client's processing. Again, therapist-centered not client-centered thinking.

T-EMDR therapists take their directives from Francine Shapiro.

> We all want the same thing. We want healthy, happy clients that can bond and love and connect. That's what we want, but seeing them with a smile on their face at the end of the session is not it (Shapiro, 2003). [That's not EMDR.]

In the words of Steve Jobs, "If you want to make people happy, sell ice cream." If you want to have fun, there is a place down the road from me called Disney World. Go there. However, if you want to transform a person's life to their true purpose, hold on to your hat, because the road is treacherous at times. Nevertheless, it is in the service of helping them reach their authentic purpose and their true self. There is no greater reward than watching that happen right in front of your eyes.

Difference Number Five: *T-EMDR therapists NEVER EVER read scripts.*

It is surprising that this problem even exists, but it does exist. T-EMDR therapists NEVER read scripts to their clients. They do not have to read anything because they know the model, history, and research in excruciating detail. They can explain EMDR to a neuroscientist in a way that makes sense to them, and they can explain it to a four-year-old in an understandable way. The therapist must know and trust the process. The client is being asked to think of the most horrific moment in their life and trust that they will safely return from that memory. Reading implies that you do not know or understand EMDR yourself. You have to read it.

How can you expect your clients to trust you if you are looking down at a script as you read to them? Trust me, once a therapist starts reading, the client stops listening. You can read a script to learn the information, but you must put it into your own words to make it your own. Explaining EMDR in your own words is not achieved by memorizing someone else's scripts but rather by understanding the material and expressing it in your own words, based on your own experiences. It does not matter if it is not perfect. What matters is that you are authentic.

Reading scripts is what amateurs do. This would be like attending a Broadway play where the actors are reading from the script, ensuring they get every word right. That sounds ridiculous. So does reading to a client.

Another problem with reading a script is that you will never know the material. You may already know how to explain it without reading it, but you will never know because you just read the same script to every person who walks in the door. This is another example of not following the client. As you read, you cannot tell if they understand. You are not talking to them; you are reading at them. Even if you have no desire to become a T-EMDR therapist, please explain EMDR to the best of your ability without reading scripts. You might be surprised by how much you already know. Remember, the client doesn't know anything, so they will not correct you if you forget something.

If you struggle without a script, use the Feynman Technique for learning. Study the material. Write it in your own words and explain it to a child without jargon.

Difference Number Six: *The Transformational EMDR therapist's primary goal is to create a self-healing environment.*

Self-healing consists of two elements: First, the therapist follows the client, as we have said, and second, the therapist creates an environment that allows the client to be in a state of flow. It is this flow state where the self-healing power of the human psyche is accessed. These two components must be established as the foundation for Transformational EMDR.

Shapiro states that one of the EMDR therapist's primary roles is to create an environment that facilitates the client's self-healing power, which they possess. Shapiro mentions self-healing more than fifteen times in her text *Eye Movement Desensitization and Reprocessing (EMDR) Therapy: Basic Principles, Protocols, and Procedures.* The T-EMDR therapist knows to stay out of the way and preserve the state of flow at all costs. In Transformational EMDR therapy, we create the state of FLOW, which is the optimal human experience of creativity and healing.

Flow allows the client to access the self-healing power of EMDR by tapping into what Michael Meade calls their inner genius, or what Jung calls the collective unconscious, or you may call it the higher self or the transcendent self. Whatever you call it, there is one thing that will prevent this access, and that is thinking. The therapist is to sit back once the flow is created. It is imperative that the therapist stay out of the way, stop thinking, and let the transformational power of EMDR take effect.

First, T-EMDR therapists absolutely do not interrupt with unnecessary questions. T-EMDR therapists never ask questions unless it is to break a loop or block. Those are the only two reasons for questioning. Questioning breaks flow. If the therapist can keep quiet and maintain flow, the client has access to their inner creative genius. The answer is within the client, not the therapist.

Second, refrain from taking notes while the client is processing. You cannot take notes and be attuned to the client. It is impossible. The therapist should also be in a state of flow, and this is impossible if you are taking notes. T-EMDR requires in-depth focus on the client. It is as if what they are experiencing right in front of you is the only thing that matters in the world, and that is precisely how it should be for both client and therapist, who are in a state of flow.

> Yes, the relationship is important. You are the pillar. You're the linkage. You are the one that put[s] this golden protective bubble around the two of you so that you can connect (Shapiro, 2003).

More on note-taking

You can keep a notepad nearby in case something unexpected or essential happens, but do not feverishly write down every client response. Your EMDR skills degrade significantly if you write down notes while administering EMDR. This detrimental effect of note-taking is a scientific fact.

Johann Hari, in his book *Stolen Focus*, quotes Earl Miller, a neuroscience professor at MIT, who tells us that there is no such thing as multitasking for humans. You might think you're multitasking, but you're not. Humans cannot multitask; only computers can do that. In fact, "multitask" was a term developed in the 1960s to describe what computers do—not humans. Humans "switch" from one task to another. Scientists tell us that switching degrades your ability to focus. If you cannot focus, you cannot attune to your client.

Three ways switching degrades concentration: The first way is known as "the switching cost and effect." Essentially, this refers to the time it takes to return to your original task after switching to another one. This back-and-forth is not a seamless process. The brain has to think, "Where was I?" and try to figure that out. This cost is compounded with each interruption.

If you are switching from taking notes to administering EMDR therapy and then back to taking notes, you cannot see the often subtle information the client is conveying. You are not attuned, and most likely, the client senses your distraction.

The second way switching degrades focus is called "the screw-up effect." When you engage in switching, you make mistakes that you would not make if you were not switching. Switching increases mistakes.

The third, and perhaps most crucial, loss during switching is called the "creativity drain": When you switch from writing notes to administering EMDR, you cannot engage in deep thought, so creativity is stifled. During EMDR, problems often need to be solved on the fly, often creatively, but you are cut off from everything you know because you are taking notes. You are cut off from your inner genius, your collective unconscious, and your creative self because you are taking notes.

If you want to become a master EMDR therapist, please stop writing down the client's responses. You do not need to write anything down; instead, be attuned to the client and just wait, watch, and listen.

A simple way to begin attuning to the client and staying hyper-focused on them is to end each set with the client's exhalation. When a therapist uses this approach, they often start to breathe with the client, thereby becoming profoundly connected to their experience. Timing the sets to the breath is a simple yet powerful technique. It is a simple way to begin to build that "golden protective bubble" that Shapiro talks about.

Difference Number Seven: *The Transformational EMDR therapist is aware of the behavioral aspect of the transformational core belief.*

They know that an *I don't matter* person takes care of everyone and never thinks of themselves. They know the *I'm not good enough* person tortures themselves by overworking because they have to be perfect. After all, if they are perfect, then they are good enough. Perfection is impossible. They understand the six stages of transformation that the client will go through. They also know how to help the client navigate this dramatic change. We will describe examples of how this is done as we proceed through this book.

Difference Number Eight: *T-EMDR therapists are self-aware.*

T-EMDR therapists who are on my team have done and continue to do their own transformational work. It is not uncommon that when we do an EMDR training and we all get together, someone inevitably begins talking about a dream they had, and a discussion ensues. Because this is a non-disease model and no one has a mental health diagnosis, EMDR is often provided among our community of Transformational EMDR therapists.

This community of therapists does not take itself too seriously. Those of us who are not good enough have resolved that negative cognition and are not afraid to answer questions with, "I do not know the answer to that." We also have a sense of humor, and often it is self-deprecating. Additionally, as consultants, we are not there to judge. The role of the T-EMDR therapist is to create a calm and safe environment so people are comfortable enough to make mistakes without fear of embarrassment. Because the work on self is essential, there is a calm and easiness about being around these people. The T-EMDR therapists are lovely people with solid boundaries and are protective of those whom we train and teach. Just like with our clients, we meet them where they are. We meet the trainees and consultees where they are.

If you are not willing to do your own work and explore the magnificence of the human psyche, how on earth can you ask your client to? Being a T-EMDR therapist is not easy, nor is it a nine-to-five process. It is a twenty-four seven experience. They do not call it a calling for nothing. We did not choose to be therapists. Therapy chose us.

Chapter 3

Flow

The Self-Healing Access to the Inner Genius

Dr. Andrew J. Dobo

Perhaps the renowned writer Ursula Le Guin captures the process of Transformational EMDR in just a few words. I subscribe to Charles Bukowski's idea that an intellectual takes something simple and makes it complicated, but an artist takes something complicated and makes it simple. Le Guin penned her short, powerful poem in her Earthsea Trilogy. It captures the power and process of Transformational EMDR.

> *Only in silence the word.*
> *Only in darkness light.*
> *Only in dying life:*
> *bright the hawk's flight on the empty sky*
> (Le Guin, 1972).

The Transformational EMDR process occurs without much talking. Hence, only in silence is the word. The process is often about emerging from a state of confusion about the client's situation that seems insurmountable. In this quiet darkness, the words come, and so does the answer to the problem.

EMDR creates FLOW, which is the ultimate human creative state of mind in which the unknown is revealed and understood. Finally, the EMDR process helps the client dismantle the old way of thinking to make room for the new way. The dismantling marks the death of the old self, making way for the new, authentic self to emerge. Hence, only in dying life. Bright the hawk's flight on the empty sky. The symbol of beginning a new life, soaring to new heights unencumbered by the past. Tethered to nothing but free flight.

What is flow?

Hungarian-American psychologist Dr. Mihaly Csikszentmihalyi discovered the concept of flow. He was a contemporary of B.F. Skinner—Skinner, who said humans seek pleasure and avoid pain. Csikszentmihalyi thought there was more to humans than that, so he studied painters and realized they would often get lost in their work. They would not eat; they would lose track of time. They were focused entirely on the creative task at hand. He called this FLOW. They painted with little reward. The reward was the human experience of being in a state of "flow." He describes it as *the optimal human experience.*

Several factors contribute to creating flow. Csikszentmihalyi tells us that the force of entropy motivates us and is more potent than the idea of discovery and creativity. We feel pleasure when we are comfortable and relaxed. We enjoy sitting in our comfy chair or couch, wrapped in a warm blanket, watching TV, or reading a book. In contrast to doing nothing, humans also crave discovery and creativity. Csikszentmihalyi discovered that these two dynamics are at war within most of us (Csikszentmihalyi, 1990). Poet and author Charles Bukowski's simple sentence described Csikszentmihalyi's discovery perfectly when he wrote, "My laziness is at war with my ambition."

Most people fall into the category of entropy, preferring relaxation over discovery and creativity. With some people, however, creativity and discovery are stronger. Ringo Starr of the Beatles talks about how they were able to write so many great songs in such a short amount of time. He attributes it to Paul. Ringo explains, "John, George, and I would be quite happy hanging out and chatting over a cup of tea all day, but Paul would always call us back into the studio. The phone would ring, and we all knew it was Paul calling us back into the studio." Paul was more attracted to discovery and creativity. The others are more on the entropy side.

Pat Metheny, a jazz guitarist, band leader, and composer, recognizes the fine line between obsession and mental health. He quotes his friend and bandmate, Steve Rodby, as saying to Pat, "You are obsessively productive." Pat again falls into the discovery and creativity side of Csikszentmihalyi's equation, having written and recorded more than twenty-five albums and played on countless others.

So, what does this all have to do with EMDR? EMDR might be the most novel way to immerse a person in that creative state of flow. That state where they have access to 20,000 bits of information per second, not just forty bits per second (Voss, 2025). Entropy is not present during EMDR processing. EMDR immediately creates a state of mind that fosters creativity. Bilateral stimulation has an incredible ability to put the person into a creative state of flow immediately. Once in the self-healing state, the client finds their truth by accessing their creative self. In EMDR sessions, it does not matter if you are on the entropy side or the creativity side. EMDR puts the client in a state of flow if the client is willing to allow it to happen. Let us take a closer look at other components of flow.

In flow, the person receives immediate feedback while engaged in the creative task. The musician knows immediately if the note played is the right one. The chess player knows after each move if his strategy is working. With EMDR, the client senses immediately if there is a move from one place to the next or if it has stalled.

In EMDR therapy, "flow" is achieved when the client is fully engaged in the creative task at hand without any interruptions. It is the ultimate monotasking experience. The task should be meaningful to the client, challenging enough to keep them on the edge of their ability, but not too difficult to discourage them.

Requirements of flow during EMDR

First, flow requires a challenge but not an overwhelming challenge. It has to be within the person's grasp. It has to be rewarding and create a sense of accomplishment upon completion. If the task is too easy, it is not interesting; if it is too hard, far beyond the person's skill, they feel hopeless and give up. A meaningful challenge is required for flow. EMDR, almost without exception, creates a meaningful challenge for the client.

Secondly, being mono-focused on the task at hand is also required. One cannot be distracted or attempt to multitask and expect to find flow. It cannot be done. Flow requires intense concentration on a single task. Flow happens in the present moment. It is completely present-focused moment by moment. There is no worry of failure. "The reason that failure is not an issue is that in flow, it is clear what has to be done, and our skills are potentially adequate to the challenge" (Csikszentmihalyi, 1990).

Thirdly, and perhaps implied in the first two requirements, is that the task must matter to the client. They have to care about the task enough to want to accomplish it.

Self-consciousness disappears because the self-expands through the act of self-forgetfulness. The EMDR therapist instructs that you do not have to understand or remember what is happening. You just have to let whatever wants to happen, happen. The ultimate living in the moment.

Flow causes the person to lose all sense of time. The painter is lost in a state of flow, does not eat, and is uninterested in the passage of time. The only thing that matters in the world is the task at hand. When they stop to catch their breath, they realize eight hours have flown by. EMDR clients often find themselves surprised when the session ends, as they have become so immersed in the process that they lose all sense of time. Steven Kotler explains the neurology of flow below. It is essential to note that he asserts flow is the only human experience in which all six motivational neurotransmitters are released simultaneously.

Neurochemistry of human experience and flow

Steven Kotler tells us in his book *The Art of the Impossible*, "When we play, the brain releases dopamine and oxytocin, two of our most crucial 'reward chemicals.'" These are pleasure drugs that make us feel good when we accomplish, or try to accomplish, anything that fulfills a basic survival need. Dopamine is the brain's primary reward chemical, with oxytocin a close second. Yet serotonin, endorphins, norepinephrine, and anandamide also play a role. The pleasurable feeling created by each of these chemicals drives us to act, and if that action is successful, it reinforces the behavior in memory. Moreover, neurochemicals are specialized (Kotler, 2021).

He goes on to say that flow may be the only human experience in which all six motivational neurotransmitters are released simultaneously in the brain.

> Flow may be the biggest neurochemical cocktail of all. The state appears to blend all six of the brain's major pleasure chemicals and may be one of the few times you get all six at once. This potent mix explains why people describe flow as their "favorite experience," while psychologists refer to it as "the source code of intrinsic motivation" (Kotler, 2021).

Destroying flow

Flow is easy to create and maintain in a typical EMDR session, yet the flow state is rarely discussed in training, nor do trainees learn what flow is or why it is so essential to maintain and establish. T-EMDR therapists understand flow is vital. They are trained to establish and sustain flow as one of their primary roles as an EMDR therapist.

The simple way to maintain flow is to refrain from asking unnecessary questions during the EMDR stimulation phase. Ironically, clinicians are often the most notorious culprits who destroy flow. They seem to be unable to help themselves from unnecessarily interrupting their client with unnecessary questions or comments.

Ryan Terry, one of the contributors to this book, shares a story where he shared his accurate observation with the client but the client did not want to hear it. He wanted to get there himself. This is a prime example of why you should keep your brilliant observations to yourself and allow the client to have their own ah-ha moment rather than you stealing their moment from them.

> One principle we emphasize in EMDR training is allowing clients to discover their own meaning within the process. This can be challenging for new therapists, especially when the material feels powerful or even mystical. Precisely because of that, it's essential to stay out of the client's way. One of my earliest EMDR cases taught me this lesson better than any lecture could.
>
> The client was someone I had previously seen for talk

therapy. He returned, open to trying EMDR, and after an unexpectedly transformative first session targeting addictive behaviors, he agreed to let me record the next one for consultation with Dr. Dobo.

In Phase Three, he selected a target related to a painful argument with his family in Boston, which had led him to move to Florida with his girlfriend and newborn daughter. He hadn't spoken to his family since. As Phase Four began, I watched him fighting back tears, jaw clenched, gripping the paddles so tightly his knuckles turned white.

Moments later, his body suddenly softened. He exhaled a long, deep breath. I paused the stimulation and asked, "What are you noticing?"

"There are these black lines leading me somewhere, toward something I need to find buried in the sand."

"Like a treasure map?" I asked, unable to hide my curious excitement.

"No," he said flatly.

"Okay ... go with that."

A minute later: "It's like X marks the spot. I need to dig for this."

"So it is like a treasure map?" I asked again.

"No. It's not a treasure map."

"Okay ... go with that," I said, confused but trying to stay out of the way.

A few minutes later: "I need a shovel to find what has been waiting for me this whole time. I finally found it."

"So you found the buried treasure."

"Nope. It's not that, Ryan."

That was the moment I understood: I needed to stop talking. The truth is his. It doesn't need my interpretation.

He continued processing, and at the end of the session he thanked me. A week later, he flew to Boston and reconciled with his family. Around the holidays, he sent me a card with a photo of his daughter in his mother's arms. On the back he had written, "Thank you for helping me find what I really treasure, after all."

This time, all I said back was, "You're welcome. Thank you, and congratulations."

He helped me find something I needed too.

EMDR is client-centered. EMDR therapists should follow the client, but often, they have their ideas about what should happen and when it should happen. Their lack of patience causes them to intervene rather than letting the client discover what needs to happen and when it needs to happen. Their lack of patience causes them to jump in with a meaningless question that immediately destroys the self-healing power of EMDR by disrupting the flow.

T-EMDR therapists are comfortable "not knowing" what is going on. They know the client will reveal it through the EMDR process. As we say, "You must trust the process," especially in those moments of doubt.

The EMDR therapist should not say anything except the query, "What are you noticing?" followed by "Go with that" after the response by the client, unless there is a problem that needs to be addressed. If there is no problem, do not ask questions. Do not interpret or share an insight. Do not reframe, paraphrase, or summarize. Please refrain from doing anything that takes the client out of flow. Do not ask, "Where do you feel it in your body?" or any other similar questions that will disrupt the flow. Shapiro says when a client reports an emotion, you should ask, "Where do you feel that in your body?" (Shapiro, 2018). T-EMDR therapists never do this. It immediately causes the client to scan their body to answer the question. It almost without exception disrupts flow. T-EMDR therapists rarely disagree with Shapiro, but we do here.

When you begin to establish flow and you carelessly interrupt flow, you will see it on your client's face. You will see the client come out of flow and start thinking about your questions as they search for the answer. Then you have to start again and try to put them back in the state of flow. You can see the engine go from 20,000 bits per second to forty bits per second about to stall out completely.

Flow is often destroyed by clinicians who overthink. They ask unnecessary questions because they are too involved in their own thinking and deciding what they want to happen in the session; they do not notice when the client is in flow or when they have destroyed it. If the client is processing without any issues, why ask questions? It brings them into the frontal lobe and out of flow. Not only is the flow disrupted, but you have also unnecessarily increased their time in Phase Four. These questions lengthen the period of distress they will have to endure for no other reason than to satisfy the therapist's curiosity.

T-EMDR therapists train by watching videos of themselves working. They are trained to recognize and maintain a state of flow on their taped sessions. Inappropriate or irrelevant questions or statements are easily identified during the taped session review and can be easily eliminated. The tape does not lie. Seeing is believing. The videotape shows the ridiculousness of gratuitous questions. The trainee learns fast not to ask meaningless questions.

Self-healing

Shapiro mentions EMDR as a self-healing process more than fifteen times in her book. EMDR therapists understand the process is client-centered, but rarely are we patient enough to allow the client to find their answer without stepping in to help. I use the term "help" loosely because unnecessary interference disrupts the process and often derails the client's creativity and problem-solving. Unnecessary interruptions not only disrupt "flow" in the session, but the interruption also ends access to the creative self-healing element of EMDR.

Flow opens up a portal to what Jung refers to as the collective unconscious. The therapist's words do not create or maintain flow. They disrupt it. When unnecessary interruptions occur, the power of EMDR is dramatically diminished.

Shapiro on self-healing:

> The Adaptive Information Processing Model is a concept of psychological *self-healing*, a construct based on the body's healing response to injury (Shapiro, 2018).

> Resolution of the disturbance is achieved through the stimulation of the client's inherent *self-healing* processes (Shapiro, 2018).

> EMDR therapy is a client-centered approach in which the clinician acts as a facilitator of the client's own *self-healing* process (Shapiro, 2018).

> The integrative AIP model underscores a methodology that stimulates the presumed *self-healing* mode of an inherent information processing system (Shapiro, 2018).

> Because of EMDR therapy's emphasis on *self-healing,* any premature attempt by the therapist to intervene may slow or stop the client's information process (Shapiro, 2018).

> I regard this healing process as an activation of a person's innate ability to heal psychologically, just as his body heals itself when he is physically wounded. A self-healing system like this makes sense (Shapiro, 2018).

> The important thing to remember is that it is your own brain that will be doing the healing (Shapiro, 2018).

Like I said, Shapiro mentions self-healing more than fifteen times in her text. These are just a few of her quotes. Self-healing occurs in flow. Without flow, EMDR's power is dramatically reduced. EMDR is self-healing, but flow is the necessary environment for the client to access their inner genius.

Power of bilateral stimulation and flow

Certainly, artists can create the flow state by being absorbed in their art. Most of our clients are not artists, and yet EMDR puts them in the state of flow almost instantly. One could write an entire book on this phenomenon.

We know as therapists that clients do not get better by what we say but rather by an internal event that they experience that changes their perception. T-EMDR therapists call this the *creative moment*. We say a stroke of genius or an ah-ha moment. Jung might say encountering the collective unconscious, or an encounter with the transcendent self of the higher self. This can only happen in flow.

Michael Meade, author and expert in mythology and stories from around the world, discusses his experience with storytelling and bilateral stimulation. He says whenever he prepares a talk, he never rehearses the story. When he speaks, he trusts that of the hundreds of stories he knows, the correct story for the moment will come to him. He trusts this process, and it has never failed him.

He discusses an internal experience that changed him. He talks about when he added drumming, which is a form of bilateral stimulation, while telling stories. He describes this experience as mystical. He felt like he was not just telling the story anymore, but he felt he was in the story itself. Being part of the story and seeing it from a new and different perspective. He said when he talks to groups, humans across cultures cannot resist the bilateral sound of drumming while telling a story. He continues and says this rhythm in the midst of a story changes all the energy in the room. It is a powerful combination of ancient rhythm, voice, and mythic images experienced at once (Meade, 2025). Within this experience, people change their perception, realize things they never thought of, and often a door to change is open for them.

EMDR does the same thing. Every one of our clients has a story. Encapsulated in their EMDR target, the first scene of the story unfolds, and the bilateral stimulation creates this ancient back-and-forth rhythm that accesses their self-healing power to see things from a new perspective. Francine Shapiro stumbled upon a lost ancient art of healing and brought it back to life for this modern age.

At its core, EMDR is bilateral stimulation paired with a story much like Meade's description of his internal experience.

Chapter 4

Transformational EMDR Approach to Phase One

Meeting the Client and Timeline as a Projective Exercise

Dr. Andrew J. Dobo

There is not much difference between the standard EMDR Phase One and a Transformational EMDR Phase One. The role induction at the first meeting is a little different and perhaps expanded because of the psychoanalytic understanding, and the possibility of engaging in transformational work is very real. The client must be informed of the often sudden and significant changes in perception and behavior that can happen after one or two T-EMDR sessions.

Phase one, as we all know, includes explaining EMDR to the new client. This explanation is tailored to the client's specific needs. Explaining EMDR to a ten-year-old is much different than explaining it to an adult. There is an additional component to the usual explanation for Transformational EMDR therapists working with adults. There is a difference between using EMDR as a disease model versus using EMDR from a non-disease-model perspective. No pathology is needed or required. Although these clients are in distress, they often do not meet the criteria of a mental health disorder.

They do not have a mental health diagnosis but feel unfulfilled and even desperate, and they do not know why. To put it simply, they are doing what they have always done. In the early part of life, these behaviors worked quite well. If you had an abusive alcoholic for a father, it made sense to be quiet, keep your mouth shut, and be invisible. This was a good way to stay safe. This was what you knew how to do. What you always have done.

Often, in midlife, the client wakes up and realizes they have been taking care of everyone, but no one is taking care of them. Nor are they taking care of themselves. Everyone in their life comes first. This behavior is the classic way in which a person who *does not matter* behaves. Around midlife, they realize something has to change; although they have no idea what the problem is, the T-EMDR therapist knows exactly what is wrong and goes to work dismantling the *I don't matter* core belief.

Below is an example of what the T-EMDR explanation during Phase One might sound like in a script. Remember, never read this to your clients. T-EMDR therapists put this in their own words.

Transformational EMDR role induction

> Transformational EMDR can cause sudden and dramatic changes in perception. It can change the way you see yourself and also the way you see others. Additionally, your

> perspective on the world will shift, and so will the way you allow the world to engage you.
>
> When there is this much change, there is often tension and difficulty. It is essential to be aware that this frequently occurs, as EMDR can lead to lasting and genuine clarity. You cannot go back to seeing things the old way, although people often try. I tell my clients that they have been living their lives from an "ignorance is bliss" position.
>
> EMDR ends ignorance and shows you what is true. The truth is not always easy to accept. Therefore, please give this matter serious consideration to ensure you're committed to undertaking this work. Clients sometimes quit their jobs, get divorced, or become estranged from family members because they realize these people have been taking advantage of them. They will sometimes break up with their boyfriend or girlfriend. Once the changes occur, they cannot be undone. You cannot undo or unknow the truth and clarity that EMDR provides (Dobo, 2016).

I like to use Prince Harry as a visible example of someone whose core belief was *I don't matter*. After EMDR treatment, he could no longer be around people who treated him like he didn't matter. The things he did and the way his family treated him will happen to your clients, albeit in less visible ways.

Prince Harry demonstrated the cataclysmic changes that can occur using EMDR from the transformational perspective. This therapy probably undid his *I don't matter* cognition and caused it to shift to *I do matter*. He found it impossible to do what he was told to do. Once EMDR causes the shift from *I don't matter* to *I do matter*, you can no longer do what you are told—unless you want to do it. You will no longer do what everyone expects of you unless it serves your true self. You will no longer be able to put everyone's needs ahead of your own.

Prince Harry gave up his family, his country, and a kingdom. He quit his job and moved to an entirely new country to figure out what his true purpose was, because following others' instructions was no longer possible for him.

This kind of thing happens to Transformational EMDR clients. It will not be as public as Prince Harry's, but your clients will face similar decisions. They will quit their jobs, leave friends and family, and find their true life's purpose, so the client must be warned. Prince Harry's example is a compelling way to illustrate the transformative power of EMDR. Harry said EMDR saved him. His countrymen, pundits, and even family call him spoiled, when in reality, he is the true hero of his family. He is living a life where he is not "The Spare" any longer.

This explanation highlights a significant difference in the explanation of T-EMDR versus the standard EMDR explanation. The effects of Transformational EMDR are explained, where, in the disease model of EMDR, this is rarely necessary because the goal is not transformation. It is simply to eliminate symptoms.

Another difference is that the client must do a list of distressing events. You may know this as a trauma timeline. The term trauma timeline is never used by the T-EMDR therapist. It is described as a list of distressing events. This list reveals the client's core belief(s). The "list of distressing events" approach offers a comprehensive overview of the client's history.

Why does the T-EMDR therapist refrain from calling it a trauma timeline? First, it is not on a line; it has nothing to do with time. This list will reveal a thorough understanding of the client's life including their negative core belief without being overly intrusive. A regular intake will provide symptomatic information. The list shows the client's core negative cognition, which is not always evident from the biopsychosocial. For the remainder of this book, if you see the word timeline, it is interchangeable with a list of distressing events. T-EMDR therapists use these terms interchangeably, but they understand what it means; it is a list of upsetting moments from the client's life.

Targeting the primary negative cognition/belief with EMDR therapy permanently causes the client's psyche to shift to the adaptive and opposing positive core belief. Their entire view of the world and themselves permanently changes. You can't "un-know" the truth EMDR provides.

When this shift occurs, one set of problems has been resolved, but an entirely new set of problems emerges and must be navigated, as the client's view of the world has dramatically changed. Their view of themselves has changed, as has their view of the people around them. Additionally, the way they engage with the world changes, as does the way they allow the world to engage with them. When there is this kind of cataclysmic shift in a short amount of time, there is trouble. The old schema has been destroyed, and the new one has yet to be discovered. It is an uncomfortable time. It all starts with a dozen distressing memories from their list of distressing events.

The anatomy of the list of distressing events (formerly known as a trauma timeline)

The client is reminded that they need only write a few words for each item on the list. They are reminded that it is not a biography. Just a few words are required for each event.

Although the items on the list are described as distressing, they can be traumatic, but they do not have to be. People often do not think they have experienced anything traumatic. Usually, they will minimize things that were indeed traumatic, saying things like, "That happened a long time ago. It doesn't bother me now." Some of us have been fortunate to get through life without severe trauma. Everyone, however, has moments of distress or just being upset about something. Shapiro tells us to pay attention to these distressing moments. They are as valuable as the big *T* traumas like rape, abuse, or unexpected death.

> When we first started, we had lots of clinicians who understandably saw the big *T* trauma that you needed to diagnose PTSD, and you can easily see rape, kidnapping, car accident, the big ones having a negative effect. We're trying to sensitize clinicians to, just because it's not these big criterion *A* ones, don't forget about those other experiences, those more ubiquitous ones of being humiliated in grade school, of being pushed away by Dad, of having these

> losses, of having all of these things that go through childhood. Realize they're going to have those negative effects also, and if they still have negative effects, you think of them as a trauma, because by dictionary definition, they had a negative effect upon self or psyche. Think of it as a small *t* trauma, but that doesn't make this the trauma protocol (Shapiro, 2003).

Our list emphasizes the more nuanced or distressing rather than traumatic, and it is presented as a projective exercise, not an assignment based on the client's chronological history. They can express this list in any way they prefer. The client is instructed to create a list of ten to twelve memories of distressing events. It is essential to give them a rough idea of how many memories they should write down. If you do not do this, you will sometimes get someone who brings in two memories or someone else who writes over a hundred, which happened to me. You cannot ignore the hard work the client put into their list, so telling them around a dozen memories will be adequate for our purposes.

When you ask someone to come up with about a dozen distressing memories, they often do not know where to start. T-EMDR therapists instruct the client to break their life into domains, explaining that we usually need a mom session. Even if you have the most incredible mom you really love, she probably did or said something that comes to mind that upset you. Continue with the remaining life domains. We usually need an educational session. Determine whether the clients were targeted by a bully or embarrassed in school. Any romantic distress. Then, of course, if there is any traumatic history, those traumas are to be on the list. This brief explanation is often effective in helping the client understand the task.

Then we will need a father session. If, for example, the client had an abusive alcoholic father, and domestic violence occurred, there might be hundreds of painful memories. It is necessary to instruct the client on how EMDR works. We inform them that we do not need all of these memories; we need one or two. When EMDR starts, the rest of the memories will move through their mind as they do during EMDR. We need one memory that functions as the first scene of a movie, and EMDR will cause your brain to replay the other memories like a movie playing in your head. We just need the first scene of the movie featuring you and your father, and EMDR will take care of the rest. That is why we only need one or two memories of each life area. We just need a way into that channel, to start the EMDR process.

Some clients worry that if they include fifteen memories on the timeline, they will need fifteen sessions. We explain to them that one EMDR session can resolve everything on the list. The list is just a starting point. After that, the process takes on a life of its own.

If the list is too distressing for the client to complete as homework, we can work on it together in session. Sometimes, we can simply listen for a memory or two to get started. If the list is too much for the client, we must discuss and listen to determine a target memory to begin with. We are always following the client and caring for them. Giving them the list to do as homework is ideal. Sometimes, this is too upsetting, and we have to meet the client where they are and begin where they are able.

Sample list

Husband's affair
Possible divorce
Didn't make cheerleader in high school
Private image
Miscarriage
Hate my boss
Wet my pants in kindergarten
Dad never came to my games (he drank at the bar instead)

A sample script for explaining the list of distressing events to your clients

Therapist: This is the only homework ever given to clients. To begin EMDR, I need to know about your history of distressing events. The events on this list do not have to be traumatic, but they can be. It does not have to be chronological. It is simply a list of distressing events. Like I said, these events may be traumatic, but they do not have to be traumatic, just distressing or upsetting.

As you create your list, refrain from editing what comes to mind. Just write down whatever comes to mind and add it to your list. Let me decide whether it is important. Any event that, when you think about it, evokes an internal response, even a small response, is worthy of being on the list. The fact that you are remembering it is very telling.

Do not dismiss a memory that appears in your mind's eye as you conduct this life review. That is my job to edit.

You must include some of your earliest memories. (Therapist should describe one of their own earliest upsetting memories to demonstrate why these early memories are so important.)

The therapist continues: These events should be from the past, present, and even future fears. The list is not a biography; you only need bullet points for each event—just a few words or even a single word. The idea is that I'll say a few words, and you can share a brief overview of the event in the next session. If there is something you don't want to share with me because it's too embarrassing, you can simply write "Private Image" on the list. You do not need to tell me what it is because discussing it won't heal it. All I need to know is that you have an image of the event. I do not need to know what it is. I can have a "confused understanding" of the event. I do not need to know much. Everything is going to process in your head.

Whether I know or not does not have much to do with the processing.

List of distressing events review

The review of the list of distressing events is often the most challenging session for the client. T-EMDR therapists are protective of the client during the review process. They inform the client that they do not need much information. The goal is to rate each event on the SUDS (Subjective Units of Distress) scale, a zero to ten scale where zero indicates no distress and ten indicates the most distress, or a value somewhere between zero and ten. The purpose is to identify which events are the most and least troubling. That is it. There is no discussion or exploration of the events. The T-EMDR gets a SUDS and moves on. This assessment helps the clinician and clients to know where to begin. Some clients are stable enough to begin with the most upsetting memories, while others prefer to start with less upsetting ones.

It is essential to inform the client that we will not discuss each event in detail or at all, as discussing all of these events can be dysregulating. We, as therapists, are being protective of the client to prevent them from leaving the session upset. It is essential to inform the client that it is not that you, the therapist, are not interested in the story behind each event, but rather that talking about these troubling memories can be upsetting. We can discuss them after we complete EMDR, when the memories are typically less upsetting.

Some clients are not upset by the memories on the list, and in this case, it is fine to let them talk about the events. We follow the client. If they are comfortable speaking, we listen. If it is clear that just thinking about the memory for a moment is upsetting, then we do not talk about the event.

There is a second task for the therapist. As the client shares each item on their list, the therapist is jotting down their best guess at the negative cognition for each event. There is usually more than one. They are also listening for the transformational cognition(s). Is this an *I don't matter* person or an *I'm not good enough* person? The list reveals the answer to this question.

The negative cognition for each event is NEVER discussed with the client during the list of distressing events review. There are two reasons for this prohibition. First, this begins an exploration that can potentially cause the clients to dysregulate. Any unnecessary exploration of the negative cognition can potentially upset the client needlessly.

Second, often, one session of EMDR can clear out all the events on their list. We never need a session on each event on the list. EMDR is a psychoanalytic approach, but many clinicians look at EMDR only through a systematic and logical lens. They address every item on the list, regardless of whether it remains a problem or not. They are unaware that EMDR heals via associated channels. If you have three or four items on the list with the same negative cognition, all of those memories will likely be reconciled in one session. No matter what, the rigid-thinking therapist takes everything on a list and processes it one at a time, session by session, whether necessary or not. That is not following your client. That is following your plan.

I recently worked with a clinician who had just completed his EMDR training but felt confused and unsure, so he sought me out for the EMDR certification process (which is an extended training credential). He shared a video of a timeline review that he had done with one of his clients. It was the first one he ever did, and it was a disaster. He was not sure why, but the client was extremely upset, left the session dysregulated, and never returned. Why did this happen?

During his training, he was taught to use a floatback on every timeline event during the list review, when he should have been taught to be protective of his clients and ask little or nothing during the review. With the approach he was taught, his outcome is no surprise. It was a predictable disaster. This harmful approach to a timeline review resulted in profound emotional connections with dozens of disturbing memories associated with each timeline event. This poor woman was being tortured with each event, compounded by a floatback with no way out.

The person who trained him was misinformed. William Zangwill, PhD, who taught me, invented the floatback. As a reminder, a floatback occurs when the client experiences a strong emotion or a body sensation, and you pause the processing to ask the client to close their eyes and be present with the body or the emotion. Then you ask them to float back to an earlier time when they felt that exact feeling or sensation. It often connects to a significant memory related to the present experience. I never recall William suggesting that the floatback be used anywhere except in Phase Four. Using it during the timeline is essentially the worst thing you can do to a patient. You are digging up their deepest traumatic memories and then sending them home without doing EMDR to resolve the material.

Additionally, it reveals a lack of understanding about the purpose of creating a timeline. A list of distressing events provides a starting point. Usually, we start with an event and never return to the list. The list, in a sense, starts the party. Once EMDR is initiated, the process opens up, and the T-EMDR clinicians wait, watch, and listen to what the client brings into each subsequent session.

Remember, be protective of your client. Please do not ask questions other than what their SUDS is. Then, you are to make educated guesses at potential negative cognitions, but do not discuss this with the client.

Finally, you will determine their transformational core belief by asking yourself, is this an *I don't matter* person, an *I'm not good enough* person, or do they struggle with both of those cognitions? Do not ask unnecessary questions, as you may only complete one or two items on the list. EMDR will resolve all the list events in one session if they are on the same associative channel, which is usually the case.

Example of the completed list of distressing events with negative cognitions after the completed review

Remember to get the SUDS from the client. T-EMDR therapists guess at the NC without any discussion of the NC with the clients.

Born premature—SUDS 5 per client's self-report
Potential NCs: I'm weak, I'm a disappointment, *I'm not good enough*, I'm different

Mom was afraid to hold me because I was so fragile—SUDS 5 per client's self-report
Potential NCs: *I'm not good enough*, I'm damaged, I'm different

First grade teacher hit me in front of the entire class for making a mistake—SUDS 6 per client's self-report
Potential NCs: I'm stupid, *I'm not good enough*, I'm not safe

Yelled at in Little League because I suck at baseball—SUDS 6 per client's self-report
Potential NCs: *I'm not good enough*, I suck

I never got to dress on the basketball team even though I practiced every day—SUDS 8 per client's self-report
Potential NC: *I'm not good enough*

Shameful score on SATs—SUDS 7 per client's self-report

Potential NCs: I'm stupid, *I'm not good enough*

Girlfriend in college broke up with me—SUDS 7 per client's self-report

Potential NCs: *I'm not good enough*

Failed an oral exam in college—SUDS 7 per client's self-report

Potential NCs: *I'm not good enough,* I'm stupid, I can't handle this

A friend killed themselves—SUDS 9 per client's self-report

Potential NCs: I'm to blame, I should've known, I should've done something

Went bankrupt in business—SUDS 7 per client's self-report

Potential NCs: I'm a failure

Cheated by business partner—SUDS 8 per client's self-report

Potential NCs: I can't trust, I'm stupid

In the example above, it is easy to determine the transformational negative cognition. This timeline reveals that this is an *I'm not good enough* person. He wasn't good enough the day he was born, being born prematurely. As the clinician, if you were to start with any of the *I'm not good enough* events, potentially all the other *I'm not good enough* events will be addressed and resolved in that initial session.

The death of a friend is a unique circumstance that will require its own session, but that is about the only outlier with this client. The associated connections are evident in this list. The transformational cognitions are apparent as well. Framing it as a projective list of distressing memories, divided into domains as we had previously discussed, provides us with the transformational map to initiate our six-stage process of Transformational EMDR.

Chapter 5

Transformational EMDR Approach to Phase Two

Preparation and the Detrimental Effect of Excessive Resourcing

M.H. Johnson, LCSW

In Dr. Dobo's basic training classes for EMDR, he shows a video of a client vomiting into a nearby trash can during Phase Four of a virtual EMDR session. In the video, the T-EMDR therapist calmly allowed the client to do what she needed to do, then asked her if she was okay to continue. When she replied yes, he picked up and continued processing in Phase Four.

In line with standard Phase Four procedure, the therapist then paused the BLS and asked the client what she was noticing. The client stated, "I know why I'm vomiting."

The therapist asked, "Why?"

"Because *my mother makes me sick!*"

The physical manifestation driven by her unconscious as a metaphor for her reality appears right in front of the therapist; her body held her hurt and anxiety of her mother's abuse and manipulation in her stomach. Her stomach needed to release what it held on to, so she could also release the *I don't matter* that her psyche held on to. That is transformation. If the therapist had stopped when she got physically sick, the line of communication that the unconscious had just opened would have immediately ended. Indeed, a client vomiting would likely cause the uninitiated therapist to stop. The T-EMDR therapist understands that this is the unconscious functioning as an ally, not as an adversary, and is not fazed. In fact, the T-EMDR therapist is excited because they know something wonderful is about to happen.

Notice the T-EMDR therapist does not say "Do you want to stop?" in the face of an adverse reaction like this. Instead, we say, "Are you okay to continue?" in recognition of our undue influence in our role as therapists. If we ask, "Do you want to stop?" when a client has an adverse reaction, we would be implicitly communicating to the client that her adverse reaction is too much for me, and I think she should stop. In asking, "Are you okay to continue?" the T-EMDR therapist focuses on the client's well-being and implicitly conveys the message to the client that he thinks she is strong enough to keep going. Notice the subtle yet dramatic difference in those two phrases.

In this case, the therapist persevered with the client's permission and without pushing the client beyond her limits. She wanted to feel better, she wanted to push through, and she did—physically and emotionally. Having allowed what needed to happen to happen, the client successfully transitioned to Phase Five during that session.

Subsequently, she made major life changes. The panic attacks and related stomach issues stopped. She stepped out of the dysfunction of her family system, got her education, and is living her best, self-differentiated life. She is not limping along, as Shapiro says; she is dancing (Shapiro, 2003).

This is Transformational EMDR at work in the real world with real clients.

This vignette stands in stark contrast to an experience I had at an EMDR conference. The audience was full of experienced EMDR therapists—EMDR therapists who were dedicated enough to EMDR to take time away from their practice and pay a lot of money to attend an EMDR conference. It was a room full of EMDR expertise and enthusiasm.

The distinguished speaker began with a warning. She was going to show an intense video of a client session she had in which the client reacted strongly. Anyone who was not prepared to see a client in distress should step out until the video was over.

"Wow," I thought. "This is going to be something!" I've had many clients work through panic attacks in session, clients wailing and shaking, clients curled up in the fetal position as their body did what it needed to do to process their trauma the way it was stored. Without fail, these clients got better. They were healed and made whole again.

The video rolled, starting in Phase Three. Soon, the client was in Phase Four. I took a deep breath to steady myself for her upcoming reaction that was strong enough to warrant a trigger warning to a room full of experienced EMDR therapists.

There it was. A tear rolled down the client's cheek. She gently wept, ever so slightly. The video ended.

"Wow," I thought. "That was the strong reaction? She

barely shed a tear." I turned to the therapists around me to ask what they thought.

"That was so powerful!"

"That was so impactful and so intense!"

"It was a beautiful, healing session, but what are you all doing on a daily basis, if that was intense?" I wondered to myself.

"I felt like a fish out of water," a T-EMDR therapist might hear.

After sitting through another expert session on integrating Internal Family Systems (IFS) and EMDR, which really meant doing weeks and months of IFS in the name of client preparation before implementing the EMDR model, I realized what it was.

"The curtain was pulled back," a T-EMDR therapist might hear.

EMDR therapists are often unprepared for hard client experiences, which leads us to focus on "client preparation"—really, over-preparation—while neglecting the therapist's own preparation. This means we are postponing the depth of client self-healing that Transformational EMDR allows, instead focusing on weeks or months of "client preparation" as we implement other therapeutic models. Then, when we finally implement the EMDR model, we are stopping the clients from going where they need to go, out of our own discomfort with their discomfort.

There is a paradoxical preparation problem here: client over-preparation caused by therapist under-preparation.

Client preparation

Shapiro does not advocate for weeks or months of implementing other therapeutic models in the name of client preparation. Instead, she tells us bluntly that preparation is not the processing (Shapiro, 2003). She also tells us, "Most clients need very little preparation because they are primarily intact" (Shapiro, 2003). This clearly does not apply to clients who are significantly fragmented or in active psychosis, but it does apply to the clients for whom the non-disease model of T-EMDR is appropriate.

Client preparation, according to Shapiro, "is just, can the client close down the disturbance in the session, and do they have something to allow them to close down the disturbance between sessions? If they can do that, you can process" (Shapiro, 2003).

She advises that therapists find *one* resource (not ten) that works for them (Shapiro, 2003). Of all the resources, including other therapeutic models available to therapists, a simple, safe place and/or container is sufficient before proceeding to reprocessing (Shapiro, 2003).

Shapiro further admonishes therapists to avoid "the drift" and stick with the protocol, stating, "The client has adequate resources to process if they can close down disturbance and let whatever happens, happen. You don't have to give them every resource they need for an entire life before you start processing" (Shapiro, 2003). We do not need to implement other therapeutic models before moving on to Phase Three.

Additional client preparation does not lead to greater stabilization. Instead, "Processing contributes to greater stabilization" (Shapiro, 2018). Excessive preparation prolongs the client's distress. T-EMDR therapists find one resource (e.g., a safe place) that works for the client and move on to Phase Three of the protocol. This takes about fifteen to twenty minutes for client preparation, including the explanation and installation of the safe place.

Therapist preparation

Therapist preparation, on the other hand, takes much longer. A T-EMDR therapist must be prepared to allow the client to go where they need to go during processing, however intense it may be. It also prepares the therapist to establish and maintain the flow state.

In Shapiro's words,

> Can I unite with the client? Am I feeling present and whole? Can I link with the client into one attuned unit? Can I maintain a value of compassion? If not, what techniques do I have to employ on me, because if I'm feeling anxious or worrying about the mortgage or looking at the ceiling ... The client gets it. And how do I make a decision about when they're going too far into the experience and I'm losing them, or when I have to use an interweave ... the relationship is important. You are the pillar. You're the linkage. You are the one that put[s] this golden protective bubble around the two of you so that you can connect. *It's very important who you are and what do you need to do to feel present and not afraid of what the person is going to be experiencing* (Shapiro, 2003).

Establishing and maintaining flow state requires the therapist to know the eight-phase protocol inside and out, with the flexibility to know when and how to adapt in the moment for the client. Rigidity is detrimental to flow. Rather, the therapist needs sufficient study and practice to be fully present with the client. This takes both the professional preparation of being able to engage the protocol without thinking and the personal preparation of quiet confidence.

The personal preparation of quiet confidence is developed in the therapist's own T-EMDR journey and personal meditation and/or prayer life. These elements are key in the development of the presence necessary to create and maintain flow for their clients, especially when the client experiences strong reactions. The quiet confidence of knowing one matters and is good enough allows the therapist to focus their inner energy entirely on the client.

This can be achieved by the aspiring T-EMDR therapist working as a client with an established T-EMDR therapist. Similarly, an active meditation practice and/or deep prayer life facilitate the inner quiet for the T-EMDR therapist to be able to hear the client purely, without noise of thought, ego, or fear. Our inner eye needs to be continuously cleansed to purely see and experience each individual client in flow state. A therapist thus prepared can hold flow space and allow what needs to happen to happen, however intense it may be.

These steps entail the personal preparation that is necessary for a T-EMDR therapist to allow what needs to happen to happen, so they can sufficiently answer Shapiro's pointed questions:

> Are you all right with what they need to experience, or are you going to say to them, "No, you don't have to feel that right now; no, it's okay"? Just think, *everyone has different tolerance levels, affect tolerance levels. What's yours? If you see a client feeling their disturbance, do you have the sense it's dangerous for them?* Are you telling your client, "Don't feel; be afraid of your feelings"? Are you giving them the same messages that they got early on: "Don't feel it. Don't express it. The other person will run away. The other person will think it's shameful. I'll disintegrate." All those messages that are in there. Have you cleaned them out of your system? Because *processing means the client will go where they need to go, and are you ready to let them do that?* (Shapiro, 2003, emphasis added)

If a room full of experienced EMDR therapists must be given a trigger warning for a lone teardrop, the answer seems to be no. Evidently, too many therapists are not prepared to let a client go where they need to go. Dr. Dobo's trainings are full of dramatic EMDR sessions, including wounds appearing on a client's body that Carolyn Lenz will discuss in a later chapter because that happened to her during EMDR. There are also videos of a woman wailing and a man whose upper body constantly makes sudden movements throughout his processing. Dr. Dobo normalizes these abreactions for his trainees because this is what is allowed to happen in Transformational EMDR.

The T-EMDR therapist's preparation of being intimately familiar with the eight-phase protocol in all its variations, working with an established T-EMDR therapist for their own

T-EMDR journey, and an active meditation practice and/or prayer life all work together to help the T-EMDR therapist establish a deep, healing connection with each client. This preparation also sets the stage for the therapist to be prepared to allow the client to go where they need to go. For their part, clients generally don't recognize everything that has gone into creating this depth of connection, but they know the intimacy of being fully seen and fully accepted when they experience it in the T-EMDR therapeutic relationship.

When not to resource

1. During processing

Shapiro also warns us against the excessive use of resources during processing. She tells us *not* to jump to a resource to calm a client during processing, supposedly helping the client —*or therapist*—feel better by limiting the intensity.

Shapiro says,

> You start them doing processing with something, and then as they're going through it, *you get kind of afraid of their affect a little bit*, and you *trigger a resource*, and you go into this sense of, yeah, life is good, and I'm feeling great, you know. But, you know, if you look a little closer, you see what's going on here. There's real intimacy involved here. But *you didn't let them go where they needed to go*, and where they needed to go was to go through a fear of death. *You didn't let them get there.* So you were being nice. You wanted them to

> feel better. *You* thought you had the answer, and you put a Band-Aid across some channel that they never got to. *Let them go where they need to go*, because who knows what memories lurk. Allow the clients their own associations to progress unimpeded (Shapiro, 2003).

Shapiro is telling T-EMDR therapists to stay out of the way. If the therapist interrupts with a resource when processing gets intense, we are preventing the processing of the underlying material, and the client—and therapist—may feel better in the moment, but the client will continue to suffer from the unprocessed material. This is antithetical to the process and the goal.

It is important to note that when Shapiro refers to resourcing during processing, she is not referring to the implementation of other therapeutic models. A cognitive interweave is not a Cognitive Behavior Therapy session in the middle of Phase Four. An inner child interweave is not an entire course of inner child therapy during processing. Parts work can be useful in a brief interweave, but it is not an Internal Family Systems session with simultaneous bilateral stimulation. A resource during processing can be a simple interweave (usually in the form of a brief question the therapist already knows the answer to) or, if necessary, the safe space or container.

Shapiro is clear that resourcing of any kind unnecessarily shuts down processing. She goes so far as to liken giving a resource during Phase Four as giving the client a benzodiazepine, saying, "using guided visualization affirmations or whatever techniques you're using to suppress affect is also doing the same thing ... like benzos" (Shapiro, 2003).

The client (and therapist) may feel more comfortable in the moment with a resource, but processing has stopped. Healing has stopped. Whatever remains unprocessed because of resourcing in Phase Four will need to be properly reprocessed in the future "in an undistorted manner, [using] this standard protocol; otherwise, you haven't used EMDR" (Shapiro, 2003). We are standing in the way of the client's self-healing when we improperly resource during processing.

2. End of session

Another time when EMDR therapists may be tempted to improperly resource is at the end of a client session. In consultations with EMDR-trained therapists working toward their certification, T-EMDR consultants have noticed a shift toward offering the container or safe space any time a client has not made the adaptive shift to Phase Five. In some cases, therapists have even used a safe space after a successful adaptive shift and installation of the positive cognition.

A T-EMDR therapist only uses a resource when clinically necessary for client functioning, not to make the client—or therapist—feel better in the moment. We intentionally do not shut it down with a resource at the end of the session, unless clinically contraindicated, for example, for client safety or sobriety. If the client can tolerate it, we let it go.

This fact is part of the extended informed consent that a T-EMDR therapist gives the client as part of Phase Two. We tell the client that whatever is processed in session is processed—it will no longer bother them. Whatever remains to be processed will remain—and that processing may continue after the session ends. As part of this, the client may have vivid dreams or even nightmares. When awake, they may have sudden recollections of memories that they haven't thought about for years or even decades. These may be distressing, but it is part of the process—the client should just notice them and let them pass, just as they would in session.

Suppose the thoughts, feelings, memories, bodily sensations, or images that come up outside of session are too intense for the client. In that case, they can use their safe space (or container) in the moment and also reach out to the therapist to schedule another session as soon as possible. Advised of this potentiality in advance, T-EMDR clients are prepared for whatever may come up for them between sessions.

Our clients are not weak. They are stronger than therapists often give them credit for. They are incredibly resilient. They have survived unimaginable and often, previously untold sufferings, carrying the weight of their torment since it happened, perhaps over half a century ago. They are not going to be crushed by the discomfort of a distressing memory that comes forward for processing between sessions. Indeed, they have lived with the weight of that memory for decades. Because we have told them that this might happen, they aren't taken off guard when it does. Further, they know they have a resource that works for them to "close down the disturbance," as Shapiro says—usually the safe place—because we have prepared them with it (Shapiro, 2003). When it does happen, it actually builds trust in the therapeutic alliance, for clients who rightfully struggle to trust, because we forewarned them and prepared them for it. They sometimes come into the next session, excited to tell their T-EMDR therapist about the distressing memory or dream, saying, "This happened, just like you said it would!"

"Where's your crystal ball, Doc?" a T-EMDR therapist might hear.

One caveat, related to clients who may be shaky in their sobriety or may have a different dangerous coping mechanism they might relapse into: If the client expresses that continued processing of material outside of session could cause a relapse, then we are going to intentionally shut down processing at the end of session with the safe place or container and/or utilize another resource like the DeTUR protocol, or otherwise target the negative coping mechanism to prevent relapse. We are not cavalier with our clients' safety. We meet them where they are and move forward slowly with them to keep them sober and safe.

Transformational Phase Two

Phase Two in T-EMDR responds to the paradox of preparation in current EMDR practice by offering a faster, yet deeper and longer approach. Client preparation is faster in that it usually takes fifteen to twenty minutes with the extended informed consent and installation of a safe space or container. There is no need to wait weeks or months, implementing other therapeutic models, before proceeding to Phase Three. To do so represents over-resourcing, prolongs client suffering, and is often caused by the therapist's own fear of a client's strong reaction. Rather, if we proceed to Phase Three after successfully installing a safe place, the client soon won't need resources—including the safe space. That's our transformational goal, for the client to be dancing, not needing myriad resources to live in quiet desperation (Shapiro, 2003).

Therapist preparation is much deeper and longer, entailing professional preparation in the therapist knowing the eight-phase protocol *"like the back of their hand"* (a T-EMDR therapist might hear), along with the personal preparation of the therapist's own T-EMDR journey and the cultivation of their meditation practice and/or prayer life. The client and therapist thus prepared, the T-EMDR therapist can hold flow and allow the client to go where they need to go for transformational self-healing to occur.

The T-EMDR therapist is professionally and personally prepared to let what needs to happen to happen, including strong physical and emotional reactions. They are prepared to answer Shapiro with quiet confidence, that they do not sense danger in a client's disturbance, they are not afraid of their own feelings, that they have cleaned the unhealthy messages behind a fear of feelings out of their system.

A T-EMDR therapist is prepared to let the client go where they need to go, *"to boldly go where no man has gone before,"* a T-EMDR therapist might say (Shapiro, 2003; Roddenberry, 1966). With Transformational EMDR, the client will never have to go there ever again as long as the therapist does not interrupt the journey unnecessarily.

Chapter 6

Transformational EMDR Approach to Phase Three

Leading the Client with the Negative Cognition, Then Follow

Elena Engle, LMHC

It's a critical phase, and I'm not just saying that because this is my chapter. A lot happens in Phase Three. The therapist guides the client through eight procedural steps, identifying the target, the image, the negative cognition (NC), the positive cognition (PC), the validity of the positive cognition (VOC), the emotions surrounding the target, the subjective unit of distress (SUDS), and the body sensations. EMDR clinicians are supposed to follow the client. Perhaps the VOC should have been called the VOPC because we are measuring the validity of the positive cognition; however, Shapiro decided to call it the validity of the cognition, assuming we would all know that the 1-7 scale refers to the positive cognition.

Anatomy of the negative cognition

Remember, the NC is the engine that drives Phase Four. Sometimes we are using a 500-horsepower Bugatti engine, like the unrestricted transformational cognitions. Sometimes we are using a small Volkswagen 100-horsepower engine, where we use a less robust cognition, and we may even add a limiting noun to the NC design or shorten the length of the sets depending on the client's situation.

"I" statements

An essential consideration for the NC design is that the NCs are an "I" statement. The NC is always about the client, not the perpetrator. When you ask the client to come up with a negative thought about the situation, they might say something like that. "My dad didn't protect me." That is about the dad, not the client; therefore, it is an ineffective NC. It misses the fundamental premise that this therapeutic work is about the client, not the client's father. Shapiro offers a quick antidote to correct this problematic thought. She suggests you ask the client using the following sentence stem: "What does it say about you as a person (or as a daughter or whoever) that your father did not protect you?" Then you tell the client to answer that question starting with an "I" statement. They will say something like, "I didn't matter to him," which is an excellent NC. This question, Shapiro recommends, provides an excellent NC for Phase Three.

The NC can be rational or irrational

It is important to remember that the NC can be rational or irrational. If you were in a car accident and you almost died, an NC of "I'm in danger" or even "I almost died" is rational.

Often, the client knows what they feel is irrational. That is fine. EMDR will repair this type of thinking. For example, a fifty-year-old woman was molested by her grandfather when she was four years old. She feels it is her fault because if she had not gotten on his lap, he would not have had to molest her. This is irrational; she even knows it. She may even say, "I know that is not true, but it feels true." EMDR therapists know that the NC can be rational or irrational.

NCs are always a simple and single thought

A negative cognition needs to be single and straightforward in thought for a few reasons. First, we must keep working memory in mind, and a simple, single thought helps to overtax it. Working memory is more than cognitive; it encompasses tactile, auditory, and visual aspects. A lengthy NC can cause the client to focus only on the cognitive, thus limiting the overtaxing of working memory. The NC must be a single thought.

If a negative cognition is too complex, such as "I'm never good enough for my dad at baseball," it will dilute the overtaxing component. Simplicity in the negative cognition seems counterintuitive to the overtaxing process. Shouldn't we try to overwhelm them with more rather than less? A single thought allows for more overtaxing of the other senses to occur, which is precisely what we want to happen when stimulation is initiated.

Choosing one cognition to start does not mean other cognitions won't be processed in the session. Remember, EMDR activates thoughts, feelings, images, memories, and body sensations. We want to ensure we start with a single thought in the service of overtaxing working memory, but once the process begins, we are in REM-like processing, and other thoughts and ideas will emerge during the process. Limiting at the beginning does not mean limiting throughout the process.

Feelings are not cognitions

T-EMDR therapists understand that thoughts are not the same as feelings. They know the NC always comes from the client's perspective and cannot be about the perpetrator. T-EMDR therapists know to follow the eight procedural steps within Phase Three to complete the Standard Protocol. They know that following these steps activates the frontal lobe for cognition element, the limbic system for emotions, and the medulla and cerebrum for body sensations.

Emotions masking as NCs reduce the efficiency of the process because the frontal lobe is not being activated when an emotion is used as a negative cognition. This mix-up can create an ineffective EMDR session.

The genius of Phase Three is that it gets the entire brain online, but not if you call an emotion a negative cognition. Example: If you have a target related to childhood abuse, people might choose "I am powerless" or "I am helpless" as their NC. Powerless and helpless can be experienced as emotions. I feel powerless. I feel helpless. The T-EMDR therapist honors these, but as emotions. If someone is powerless or helpless, the T-EMDR therapist knows these feelings create congruent thoughts like "I am not in control" or "I am trapped." These are better choices for the NC because they are thoughts.

This is one of the reasons why the NC is where we break the "follow the client rule." Although we listen to the client, and we may use an NC they provide if it feels correct. Remember, using feelings as NCs prevents the brain from fully reprocessing. Helpless, hopeless, and powerless often describe the feeling of the situation. There are times when it's appropriate (Shapiro, 2018), but remember, we want to activate the entire brain. You lose frontal lobe activation if you focus on the emotion. These may be fine points, but details can create a smooth and efficient session instead of a cumbersome and sluggish session.

NC design: a continuum from unrestricted to restricted

Transformational cognitions—the most unrestricted and powerful NCs

There are two transformational cognitions that T-EMDR therapists understand: *I don't matter* and *I'm not good enough*. As Dr. Dobo said at the beginning of this book, which is worth reiterating here, he attended one of Dr. Sue Johnson's trainings in Chicago, the developer of Emotionally Focused Couples Therapy. Dr. Johnson shared her research, stating that in eighty-five percent of couples, one partner is a pursuer and the other a withdrawer. The remaining fifteen percent of couples are both pursuers or both are withdrawers. Translated to negative cognitions, this means one partner is an *I don't matter* (the pursuer) person, and the other is an *I'm not good enough* (the withdrawer) person. From the moment a client reaches out to inquire about therapy, the T-EMDR therapist asks themselves, "Is the person in front of me an *I don't matter* person or an *I'm not good enough* person?" T-EMDR therapists begin to make this determination in the first minutes of meeting a client and throughout the preparation phase.

The T-EMDR therapist recognizes that transformational cognitions must be used with great care, as breaking these negative cognitions can have a profoundly destabilizing effect. If an *I don't matter* person begins to believe and know they do matter, that will change every single relationship in their life, for better or worse. They will no longer tolerate figuring things out so everyone else can be happy. They will voice their opinion on the movie they want to watch, and they will enforce boundaries to be treated more healthily. The same applies to the person who thinks *I'm not good enough*. They will no longer take the blame for everything. They might even slow their roll a bit goal-wise because they'll realize they were going at breakneck speed, and it's now okay for them to enjoy the journey; it's not just about the destination. The T-EMDR therapist is skilled at helping their clients through these stages of transformation.

Why are transformational cognitions so powerful?

First, as Sue Johnson stated, every one of us has one or both of the transformational cognitions. You cannot say that about any other NC. We all have these NCs in common as part of our human experience. Transformational cognitions develop at an early age. When children experience a distressing or traumatic event, their underdeveloped nervous system can have a drastic response. Since children are concrete thinkers, they lack the cognitive ability to consider that something may not be about them. This is why lots of children think divorce is their fault, or they are stupid if they are humiliated in grade school, or they are unlovable if their parents do not play with them. They can't think that maybe their parents were unhappy with each other, their teacher was stressed, and their parents need to work to pay the bills. Their undeveloped brain and nervous system wire together and create core beliefs. Just because these examples are not necessarily "big *T*" traumas does not mean they do not have lasting adverse effects.

I was working with a very successful adult, now retired. She lives and breathes for her family. She wants everyone to get along, eat good food, and live merrily. She reported having a great upbringing and a loving family. She reported only two recent events that she was struggling with: a recent passing in the family and a frightening medical diagnosis now in remission. So why was she having fits of rage when family members made poor choices or failed to heed her concerns? Why, after all of her successes, did she still not feel valued? We began EMDR, and things started to click: Being the only daughter, she knew she mattered. She also felt the need to take care of everyone, helping her mother with all the household chores and preparing meals. She mattered as long as she was caring for ailing parents. She mattered as long as she did what others expected her to do and needed her to do.

She also realized she would never be as good as her sibling, the Golden Child. The Golden Child got into more trouble, received poorer grades, and overall needed more help from their parents, particularly their mother. My client was capable, independent, and made wise choices. Targeting her mother's death was linked to numerous times when her mother preferred the Golden Child; targeting her cancer diagnosis was linked to multiple times when her father preferred his sons. She wasn't good enough for her mother and didn't matter to her father. That's why, after her mother died and she received her cancer diagnosis, all hell broke loose in her family because she decided to treat herself like she mattered and moved out of state with her immediate family.

She was no longer around to take care of everyone else like they mattered, and she knew she was good enough to fight cancer. Transformational EMDR helped her realize she doesn't need to be perfect: She is good enough. It also helped her realize that she sees herself in a new, positive light, that she matters. Her childhood didn't have any "big *T*" traumas. These were elementary family dynamics and societal norms that created her negative beliefs. She is now cancer-free and living up her golden years.

The reasons *I don't matter* and *I'm not good enough* are so powerful, so transformational, because they contain many other cognitions within them. *I'm not good enough* can include "I'm stupid," "I should've known better," or "I'm a failure." *I don't matter* contains "I have no voice," "I'm invisible," or "I'm unloved." Using the limiting NCs is entirely appropriate at times and may be good clinical judgment. Activating transformational cognitions can be overwhelming for the clients, but the T-EMDR therapists know that limiting cognitions narrows the amount of material to process. Let's take a look at the flow charts for a visual explanation.

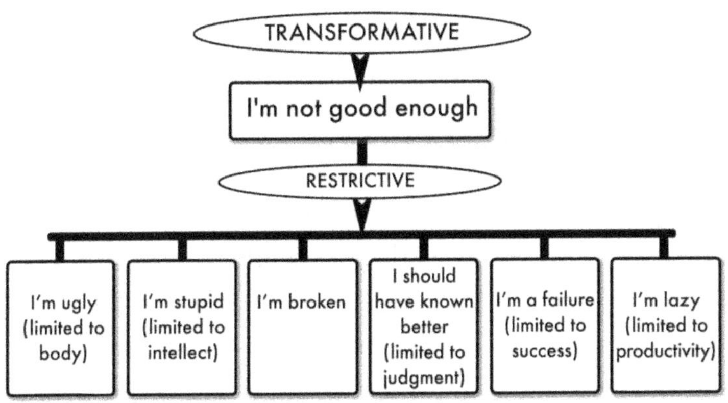

The more restrictive cognitions within the transformational cognition are in the bottom row. The restrictive cognitions reduce material. The transformational cognitions encompass all other related negative cognitions that will lead to generalization. This creates an unimpeded processing session for your client because it moves through their entire life. "It allows the full range of associations to be made throughout the targeted memory and integrated network" (Dobo, 2016).

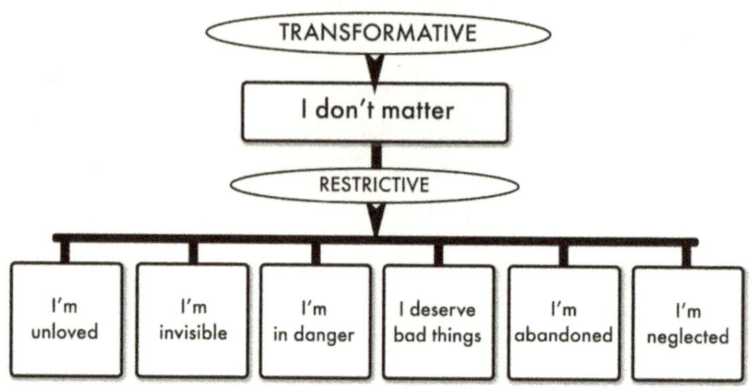

Transformational NCs cause the client to change dramatically. These cognitions change the way they view themselves and the way they view the world. They also change the way clients engage with the world and how they allow the world to engage them. These changes are cataclysmic. Dr. Dobo uses the metaphor, "It is like using a flashlight (restrictive cognitions) versus using a lightning bolt (transformational cognitions)." My counterpart, Ryan Terry, says, "It's like using a garden hose versus a fire hose." I like to harken to the cliche "less is more," by Mies van der Rohe. The T-EMDR therapist knows these two NCs simplify the process yet provide complex, permanent, and comprehensive transformation.

Simplifying the process helps the T-EMDR therapist identify individual predictable patterns in their client's lives. This is a person-centered therapy, after all. *I don't matter* people usually think of ways to make everyone else's life better but theirs. Everyone and everything else matters; they do not. *I'm not good enough* people are typically go-getters: They rise to the top of their studies and work. They continuously try to prove themselves, but their work is never done because they will never be good enough. You do not have to know very much about a client to know which NC they are. If you understand the effect of these NCs, you will gain a significant understanding of the client simply by knowing which transformational NC is driving their life.

Examples are:

- Client is adopted. *I don't matter.* (Mom disposed of me.)
- Client had alcoholic parents. *I don't matter.* (Alcohol mattered.)
- Parents always compared the client to their brother. *I'm not good enough.* (My brother is always favored.)
- Professionals with endless letters after their name. *I'm not good enough.* (See how much stuff I know.)
- Dad wanted a boy. I'm a girl. *I don't matter*, and *I'm not good enough.* (It could be both.)

Yes, an individual could be both NCs, just like in the example I gave above.

T-EMDR therapists know this can happen sometimes. It helps to ask, "Is this client not good enough *because* they don't matter? Does this client not matter *because* they're not good enough? Or are they just simply both?" I don't have the answer for everything, so I'll tell you this: It depends. The answer is right in front of you. Get to know your client, do EMDR, and the answer will present itself.

These transformational cognitions ignite the transformational process. They bring clarity to the client about the damaging and limiting effect their negative cognition has on their life. This clarity causes them to think about what has to change in their life. They start to see clearly and know they must change. This clarity can happen quickly, sometimes after just one session of EMDR.

At a recent training, a middle-aged female targeted an *I don't matter* moment in her life. After her first session at this training, she went home, quit her job, left her boyfriend, and took a new job she was previously offered but was hesitant to accept. She was thrilled by her change. Change does not always happen so quickly, but it can happen when people have been unhappy for a long time. They know something has to change but are not sure what. EMDR sometimes brings this profound clarity that makes the decision easy. The client understands and is ready to begin their authentic purpose. Timing is everything.

T-EMDR therapist follows the client except for the NC

T-EMDR therapists follow the client in all areas of the EMDR process except for the negative cognition (NC). The T-EMDR therapist leads with the negative cognition. This is the only exception regarding following the client. The T-EMDR therapist knows the negative cognition drives the session. Choosing the correct negative cognition and designing it properly is imperative. The T-EMDR therapist has an in-depth understanding of the nuances of the NC that can impact the EMDR session. Let's explore the considerations for designing the NC.

> Identifying the negative cognition assists the client to recognize more fully its irrationality, establishes a baseline, and helps to stimulate dysfunctional information that requires reprocessing (Shapiro, 2018).

Shapiro states numerous times in the third edition of her book that NCs are interpretive, not descriptive.

> While the term "cognition" has often been used to define all of the conscious representations of experience, in EMDR therapy, we use it to signify a belief or assessment. Therefore, the cognition represents the client's current "interpretation" of the self, not merely a description. As an interpretation, the negative cognition answers the question, "What are my self-denigrating beliefs about myself in relation to the event?" (Shapiro, 2018)

Shapiro further states, "the NC should represent a general statement about the self rather than about the specifics of the event" (Shapiro, 2018).

This generalization allows the client to process more material about the experience rather than just a specific episode. T-EMDR therapists listen for the generalized interpretation about the self.

Some people are immediately on board when you tell

them their core belief. I was meeting with a client, and they were sharing the reasons why they decided to come to therapy. They achieved many goals in life: higher education, financial stability, a healthy family, and more. Yet they couldn't shake this feeling that something was wrong with them. They were always very hard on themselves and wanted to be perfect for everyone and make things perfect for others. Cognitively, logically, things were perfect, but they were still miserable and could not stop the carousel of negative thoughts circling in their head.

After listening to her, I reflected her list of complaints back to her and said, "It sounds like nothing is ever good enough. All of these things you do, even trying not to be perfect, all of the efforts just aren't good enough." The client grew quiet and then solemnly said, "It's like I'm not good enough." Thankfully, I was able to provide this client hope as I guided them through their Transformational EMDR journey, and they now know they are good enough. These few words profoundly affect every area of a client's life, which will be explored in later chapters.

Another client came to see me for anxiety, a first-generation immigrant who very often found himself needing to be an interpreter for his parents and the mediator during their numerous separations. A very driven individual with high goals and even higher hopes. He was quite the meticulous planner, which allowed him to experience wonderful things but also kept him on high alert. Constant vigilance was exhausting. When he finished sharing his story, I had one question: "When do you think enough will be enough?" The idea was utterly foreign to him. He teared up. His transformational journey began when someone finally saw him—me—and permitted him to slow his pace. He didn't have to prove to anyone he was good enough. He just needed to believe it. I was honored to be his T-EMDR therapist.

Some people are not willing to immediately accept their negative cognition. I was having a session with a client. We had discussed transformational cognitions. She had immediately identified with *I don't matter*. When we met the very next week, she rejected it. She couldn't shake the question of "why me?" She wondered if maybe she wasn't enough. Perhaps she wasn't worth it. She asked if EMDR could help her know she can "get through this." She didn't want to pity herself, saying twice, "It doesn't matter." She wanted to know she would be okay. EMDR does not give you what you want. It gives you what is true. Timing is everything.

While creating the Phase Three protocol, I was unsuccessful in convincing the client that the negative cognition was *I don't matter*. However, I did notice the client said, "Bad things happen to me" three times in less than five minutes. When she said it the first time, I was still arguing for, *I don't matter*. When she said it a second time, I thought, "But bad things did happen to her, so that may not work." When she said it a third time, she was trying to explain how she doesn't want to pity herself and doesn't want to keep asking herself, "Why me?" Ah, avoidance of the transformational cognition. Okay. Time to follow the client again. Timing is everything.

Sometimes we need to shut up and let EMDR do its work. She was treating herself like she didn't matter. Dismissing her pity and denying her anger. She wasn't ready to accept *I don't matter*. By going with what she was saying,

"Bad things happen to me," shaping the NC into an "I" statement, "I'm unlucky," EMDR gave her the truth. I didn't waste time being right. I had taken the lead, said my piece, and met the client where she was. We ended the session with her knowing she can learn how to figure this out and treat herself with the same care and respect she deserves.

I hope these examples help you understand why the T-EMDR therapist's lead is with the NC. Also, as this final example demonstrates, we listen and let the client guide us. Sometimes we meet in the middle. Leading does not mean coercing. We are listening for the generalized interpretation of the target moment. The NC can expand throughout the client's entire life with a single image as the target with the proper NC design.

The T-EMDR therapist also heeds Shapiro's statement, "It is vital that this cognition stem from the client's own experience and not be an artificial construct of the clinician" (Shapiro, 2018). We are not arbitrarily labeling clients. We are waiting. Watching. Listening. We do not want just to heal the symptoms and send our clients "back to a life of quiet desperation" (Shapiro, 2003). We are looking at each individual's life history and helping our clients understand how these negative cognitions no longer have to rule their lives. We are listening intently to identify what might need to be processed to help get this person to an actualized state (Shapiro, 2003).

The T-EMDR therapist yearns for each individual to live their authentic purpose truly, to bring them to a level of healing and genuine self they didn't even know was possible. The T-EMDR therapist knows that the wrong NC can cause the process to break down, so gently insisting may be the best course of action to develop the NC together (Dobo, 2016). "The client came in because this is a complaint. Is this all I'm going to do? Or do I look at the entire picture? Because processing involves all of this. And the client won't even know it's possible unless you let them know" (Shapiro, 2003).

Since anyone reading this should be familiar with EMDR and the eight-phase model, Transformational EMDR therapists determine the rest of Phase Three as Shapiro instructs. T-EMDR therapists' difference is in the NC design. This book introduces the varied power of the negative cognitions and their design. If we look at the NC design from the most unrestricted to the least unrestricted, our continuum looks like this.

Telling the client the NC without telling them the NC

One strategic way to inform the client of their NC without debate is to paraphrase. We all know how to paraphrase. You paraphrase the situation that is being targeted. After the paraphrase, you reflect the NC to the client, and if they agree with the reflection, you have the NC, and you do not even have to discuss it further. They agreed with the reflection, and you wrote it down as the NC. It might sound like this.

"So, you were getting a big award at school. The American Legion Award. It is given to the smartest kid in the school. As they called your name, your father wasn't there; he was at the bar, where he always is. It seems like you didn't matter to him that day; alcohol mattered, and his friends at the bar mattered more than you. Does that sound right to you?"

The client responds, "Yes, that sounds exactly right."

So we just told the client what the NC is, using a simple paraphrase. This technique saves a great deal of time debating over the NC. Paraphrase and tell them the NC. This is an empathetic and time-saving strategy.

To review: NCs from most generalizable to the least

Transformational negative cognitions are the most generalizable and most powerful NCs.

I don't matter.

I am not good enough.

Next, we can add a noun to any of the transformational NCs, and this can limit the amount of material that gets processed. *I don't matter* can generalize to any moment in the client's life when they felt like they did not matter. "I don't matter to my dad." This NC will often be just about the dad and limits its generalizability. Adding a noun limits its power.

Then we can use more typical NCs that are on Shapiro's list, such as "I should have done something" or "I can't trust my judgment" etc. All of these fall under the NC of *I'm not good enough*, but they have a limited generalizability capacity. Even in the Shapiro list, some NCs have more power and some less. For example, "I am in danger," which is more robust than "I'm not safe." The "not" usually reduces its activating power. To review, the following are examples of NC designs from the most to the least generalizable.

Transformational NCs

I don't matter (most generalizable)

I don't matter to my dad (less generalizable)

Non-Transformational NCs

I'm in danger (robust)

I'm not safe (less robust)

Example two

I can't trust (robust)

I can't trust my husband (less robust)

This principle can be used on almost all NCs. It is essential to consider the generalizability of the NC. Sometimes you want unrestricted, and in some cases, you prefer to move more slowly, so less generalizable NCs are required.

I hope this discussion helps you make more nuanced choices with the NCs. The NC is the engine you are putting into your EMDR processing, so make sure you are using the proper one for the job.

Chapter 7

Transformational EMDR Approach to the Body as Phase Four Stimulation Begins

Not Only Does the Body Keep Score, It Also Speaks

Carolyn Lenz, LMHC

Phase Four of EMDR begins when the client is stimulated with bilateral stimulation (BLS) and actively processes distressing associations with the identified target. These associations manifest as any combination of all five channels: thoughts, feelings, memories, images, and physical sensations (Shapiro, 2003). However, the T-EMDR therapist understands there is also a sixth channel—unconscious material. This sixth channel encompasses associations that lie outside our conscious awareness. This material can manifest as thoughts, feelings, body sensations, images, symbols, dreams, nightmares, or metaphors. These manifestations often go unnoticed or ignored because clinicians are rarely trained to recognize and understand the language of the unconscious.

This material must be identified and addressed to achieve the transformational changes discussed in this book. In Dr. Shapiro's keynote speech (2003), she expands on the topic of transformational change and actualization, which we presented earlier in this book, but it is worth reiterating here.

> Someone comes in with a driving phobia. If I just concentrate on the driving phobia and send her back to a life of quiet desperation, I wouldn't personally consider that good work unless that's all she's willing to do, but as a clinician, if I'm taking a history and seeing the larger clinical picture, at least let me make the person aware of the possibilities and the potential to see if there's other things, because a symptom like a phobia or PTSD can simply be masking. It's like taking the quilt off the mattress. You know there can be a lot of lumps and bumps that you need to deal with, so if I take a good clinical history, I'm able to identify what might need to be processed to help get this person to an *actualized state* (Shapiro, 2003).

During Phase Four of processing, clients are often emotional and frequently experience somatization (but not always). As a clinician, it's essential that you have adequately prepared your clients for what they might experience and that you have established rapport. Hence, they trust that you will keep them safe throughout the process and that, as the clinician, you won't let your feelings about what the client is going through interrupt their own self-healing. In Dr. Shapiro's 2003 keynote speech, she states explicitly,

> Are you all right with what they need to experience, or are you going to say to them, "No, you don't have to feel that right now; no, it's okay"? Just think, everyone has different tolerance levels, affect tolerance levels. What's yours? (Shapiro, 2003)

Additionally, as a T-EMDR therapist, it is essential to understand how the body communicates in Phase Four and how to effectively navigate this information. When physical sensations or somatization are present, it can mean one of three things or ALL these things: First, it can be a metaphorical message from the body; secondly, it might be a traumatic reenactment they experienced earlier in their life; or it could just be sensations in the body brought on by processing.

These physical sensations are often referred to as "durable," meaning they persist for several sets or recur intermittently over the course of processing.

That's significantly different from an image, or even more so with a clichéd phrase that will be gone in an instant. Furthermore, physical sensations are also significant because they often link back to experience(s) that are outside of our conscious awareness. This hidden material, which we know is stored in the implicit memory system, remains hidden from our awareness and is often fragmented, confusing the client and the therapist. "Why did I get so upset over such a small thing?"

When a client experiences a physical sensation during processing, it presents an opportunity to utilize one of the bridge or floatback techniques (Dobo manual, 2018).

John Helen Watkins developed the somatic bridge technique for the clinical hypnosis community. William Zangwill, PhD, developed the floatback technique for the EMDR community. Both methods are administered similarly. Both take a present expression of the body or emotion and connect it to the source of the sensation—a powerful tool for the EMDR therapist.

The technique works by "bridging" a present experience of distress to a time in the past when they experienced something similar. When the bridge connects to a previous experience, the identified event is often unconsciously associated with an implicit memory fragment (Dobo, 2018). Frequently, these are not items that ever came up on the timeline or that the client would logically think are connected to the present-day distress.

As a T-EMDR therapist, you understand the answer is never in the frontal lobe. The material is stored implicitly, and by the very nature of implicit memory, it is hidden. It is beyond our conscious awareness. These unconscious associations are often powerful and act as feeder memories to the current distress. The T-EMDR therapist understands that by accessing these unconscious associations and working through them, we are facilitating a more complete healing.

The floatback or bridge begins with an implicit memory fragment, which is often a somatization; for example,

"My throat is tight."

"My chest feels heavy."

"I feel nauseous."

This fragment then connects to an earlier memory, thus filling in the fragmented story. This technique bridge connects the present to the past, and the memory in its entirety is revealed; EMDR continues, and the problem is healed.

In most EMDR sessions, there is an opportunity to use a somatic bridge/floatback (Dobo, 2018). When using a somatic bridge/floatback, it is critical to obtain the client's consent to try it and, if they choose to, to explore the memory it connects to. If the client does not feel comfortable going with that memory, reassure them that it is okay. Take note of this experience, as it is worth discussing in Phase Eight, and determine if it needs to be targeted in the future. Additionally, somatization during processing may not be linked to a specific event or experience; in such cases, proceed with the standard protocol.

For example, I was working with an adult male who initiated treatment due to social anxiety. We were making progress in EMDR on a target related to recent anxiety when the client started to have somatization. While processing, I noticed that his throat was becoming very flushed. This is not something that I had noticed in previous processing sessions, so I was curious about what might be going on for him. I let a few passes go by and then stopped and asked the query. He reported feelings of fear and anxiety, so we went with that. Please note that although I was curious about somatization, I did not ask him about it or direct him to notice it. Instead, I continued to follow his process and let him go where he needed to go.

As he resumed processing, his throat continued to flush more, but now, with some white blotches on the side of his throat, his body posture was quite tense. When queried, he reports some tension in his upper body and tightness in his throat. Now, we have significant activation of body sensations, so I suggest a somatic bridge. With his consent, I invited him to close his eyes and notice those sensations in his throat and upper body, then see if he could "float back" to a time in the past when he had those same sensations.

He closed his eyes and spent some time with the sensations, then his head jerked back, and he opened his eyes. He shared, "It felt like this when my father pinned me against the wall and choked me when I was a kid." I asked him if he was okay with that memory, and he said yes; BLS was immediately resumed, and this significant moment of abuse he experienced had never come up in our history-taking, timeline, or previous sessions. As a T-EMDR therapist, this does not surprise me because the answer is never in the frontal lobe. The material is stored in the implicit memory system beyond our awareness. All this excessive inquiry is often a waste of time. EMDR reveals what needs to be processed, not the client's frontal lobe. It is EMDR that has the power necessary to uncover the truth.

This example demonstrates the breakdown of the adaptive information processing model and an expression of an implicit memory fragment. It is fragmented because the client has no idea why they are experiencing these emotions. The somatic bridge connects the present to the past, and the memory is healed in its entirety.

The body was speaking through the tension, flushing, and blotchy spots, which were in line with where a hand might apply pressure to one's throat. When the client revisited that memory, he experienced a cathartic release of emotion and closure on an experience that had been remembered but without any accompanying emotion, somatization, or vivid imagery.

Another type of bridge that a therapist might use when the body speaks is called the proprioceptive bridge/floatback. This strategy is used when a client moves their body into an unusual or significantly different position or posture during processing.

An example of this occurred when I was working with an adult client on an insect phobia. They were seated in a chair and, during processing, exhibited jerking motions of the upper body, twisting at the waist almost to look over one's shoulder. A proprioceptive bridge/floatback was completed, and the client connected to a memory of her being across her father's knees, pants down, and being continually hit. She had repeatedly attempted to reach behind herself to protect her bare skin from his painful strikes. This movement exactly mirrored the involuntary twisting of her upper body that occurred during processing. I fully believe we could have done talk therapy for the rest of eternity on this phobia and never connected this earlier trauma that was activated when she saw an insect. However, with the use of proprioceptive bridge/floatback during EMDR, we were able to accomplish it in minutes and fully resolve the phobia and underlying trauma.

Again, this does not surprise me because, as a T-EMDR therapist, I have learned to accept that "I do not know," and I am aware that the client also does not know. However, together, EMDR will show us how to heal the problem. As a T-EMDR therapist, I have learned to let the client speak to me. This language uses words sometimes, but often it is not words. Understanding this wordless language took a little getting used to.

The floatback and bridge interventions are potent ways to let the unconscious speak as it guides us, without words, to where we need to go. I have dozens of stories like these. Once

I accepted the reality that *I do not know*, my own observation and attunement to the client and my ability to be in a state of flow dramatically improved. I learned that all I have to do is to wait, watch, and listen.

When you notice a posture change happening, the first thing you want to do is stop the BLS and ask the client, "Can you please freeze in that position?" Then, you can invite the client to try the proprioceptive bridge/floatback to an earlier time when they were in that position. If they connect with a memory, ask if they would like to explore it further.

A second example of this is when Dr. Dobo was working with an adult client. Suddenly, during processing, both her legs extended straight out in front of her. The proprioceptive bridge/floatback was completed, and the client connected to being a young child sitting on the couch with her feet extended straight in front of her (due to her small size).

Another common way the body speaks in Phase Four is through traumatic reenactment. A traumatic reenactment occurs during the active processing of distressing material. The client may physically manifest aspects of the physical symptoms or damage that happened during the original experience. Traumatic reenactments might show up as an asthma attack, bruises, unconsciousness, or something else that occurred physically during the traumatic experience. Don't worry; someone's arm isn't going to break when you are targeting the trauma of breaking an arm in an accident, but it's possible that bruising or other physical aspects of the event could.

I experienced a traumatic reenactment when processing a target related to child abuse I experienced. During the actual event, I was repeatedly hit on my legs, choked, and eventually passed out. I targeted this experience in an EMDR session and fully resolved it. However, later that night, when I changed clothes, I found my legs spotted with bruises, welts, and handprints. These markings had not been there earlier that day and were clearly a traumatic reenactment as it was cleared from my body using T-EMDR. Although seeing the bruising was confusing and alarming, it also gave me a depth of empathy for my younger self that went far beyond what I understood prior.

During the processing session, I had cycled through a multitude of memories associated with the negative cognition, "I'm trapped." Not just abuse, but jobs, chronic health issues, car accidents, relationships, etc.

The processing was intense and rapid, and then suddenly I got a horrible pain in my left calf. The pain felt like I had been struck by a lightning bolt and seemed to come out of nowhere! I doubled over, grabbing my calf and apologizing for interrupting the process (BLS was abruptly stopped due to my sudden reaction). The therapist reassured me it was okay to take my time to stabilize and simply "waited, watched, and listened." I rubbed my leg for a minute or so, thinking I had never felt pain like this and feeling confused about what had happened. Eventually, it subsided, and I stated I was ready to resume processing.

Wisely, the therapist asked if I could acknowledge that sensation in my leg. I said yes, and BLS was resumed. Instantly, it linked to the target memory, that moment when I was trapped in a room with my abuser, fighting for my life. However, this time, I was an adult! I quickly rescued my younger self from the room, cared for her, and took her to a safe place. Then I went back to the room, where I locked my abuser in so she could never torment me or anyone again. The SUDS immediately dropped, and we moved into Phase Five, fully resolving the target. I was elated and felt amazing! Honestly, what had happened with the pain in my leg was not even a thought in my head when I left that session.

Several hours later, the bruises I found included one on the back of my left calf (where I had felt the sudden and intense pain during Phase Four). These markings had not been there earlier that day and were clearly a traumatic reenactment.

Likely, the sudden pain I experienced in my leg (that I couldn't logically understand) was a fragmented implicit memory of the pain and damage that I experienced during that incident of abuse. As the sensation and experience were bridged, it was released from my body and consciously integrated as an experience I had survived rather than an ongoing threat. The past was no longer present, and the trauma was healed in its entirety.

Even though the therapist did not use the formal somatic bridge/floatback technique, he clearly recognized somatization and the potential to explore this. He followed my lead perfectly, pausing to allow me to stabilize when I needed it (without questioning me, comforting me, or breaking the flow state), then asking for my consent to proceed with that sensation when I was ready to resume. Even though neither of us knew what had happened or what it meant, we did know that the body was speaking and that EMDR would show us what needed to be healed. That's precisely what it did.

Traumatic reenactment remains an area of emerging research, both within the EMDR community and the medical community. Due to this, I emailed Dr. Bob Tinker to get his perspective on how and why traumatic reenactment occurs. Dr. Tinker has been a practicing EMDR therapist for well over thirty years, is a pioneer in this field, and is the leading researcher in traumatic reenactment. In the emails we exchanged, Dr. Tinker shared that, in over thirty years of doing EMDR with clients, he had about ten cases of "stigmata" (the term he uses for traumatic reenactment) (B. Tinker, personal communication, May 21, 2025). He then expounded further on his understanding of how and why traumatic reenactments manifest.

Dr. Tinker states:

> With my clients, it (stigmata) seemed to appear in the middle of a course of EMDR when we focused on a traumatic event that involved physical or sexual abuse, and as the traumatic event resolved, the stigmata stopped occurring. If it recurred, I took it that the trauma was not fully resolved, and [we] would go back to work on it some more. The way I came to understand it, EMDR broke down the dissociations that caused the markings not to heal. When the dissociations broke down completely, the marks would heal and not reappear. Another way of saying this is that the abuse had to occur often enough that the victim was able to dissociate before the abuse occurred (B. Tinker, personal communication, May 21, 2025).

Dr. Tinker identifies important factors that seem to consistently be present in a traumatic reenactment: physical injury to the body during the original trauma; the victim was able to predict the potential for injury/trauma and dissociates *prior* to the event; and finally, when all dissociated aspects are integrated, the body releases the stigmata and thus heals itself. The factors that Dr. Tinker outlines as the ingredients to a traumatic reenactment are precisely what I faced and deeply helped me understand my own experience. Specifically, he states: "In your case, I think that the stigmata coming up again after ten years is an indication that the trauma was not fully resolved (as you indicated) and that the therapeutic setting was safe enough to work on it again" (B. Tinker, personal communication, May 21, 2025). Although previous EMDR processing had significantly helped decrease the distress for this event, it was not until the final piece clicked into place (the shift from NC: "I'm trapped" to the PC: "I'm free") that my body physically released the dissociated injuries so they could finally heal and fully resolve this trauma.

The type(s) of disassociation that Dr. Tinker identifies as a component for traumatic reenactment are more in line with what a client with a Dissociative Identity Disorder (DID) or other clinical dissociative condition(s) might experience. This type of dissociation is significantly different from the usual dissociation that often occurs *during* a traumatic experience. The latter is relatively common with trauma, results in some fragmentation in memory networks, and is not likely to cause a traumatic reenactment when fully reprocessed. This differentiation helps us understand why disassociated or fragmented material often becomes conscious in EMDR but does not relate in a traumatic reenactment.

During a Jungian training in which Chapter 16 author Ryan Terry assisted Dr. Dobo, Ryan got an urgent request for a FaceTime call. It was from a colleague Dr. Dobo had trained, Drew Breznitsky: "Please call me now!"

Ryan resisted a little. "Drew, we are in the middle of training."

Drew persisted. "Call me now. Trust me, Dr. Dobo will understand."

Ryan called Drew. Drew recounted a session he just had where he watched a woman's wrist start to manifest cuts and bleeding during Phase Four. Fortunately, Drew knew to continue processing as long as the client was willing to do so.

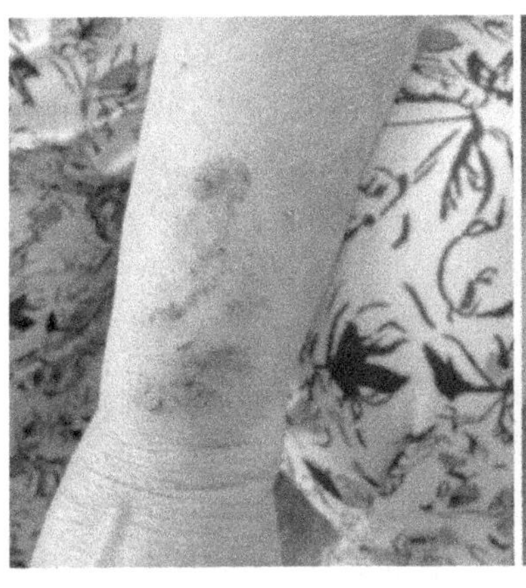

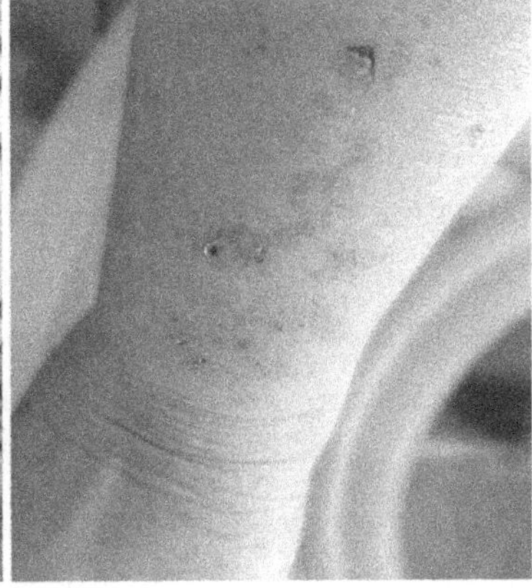

The target was chronic sexual abuse. This woman, now in her sixties, was tied up as a child and raped by a brother from early childhood through adolescence. Like the previous situations, she most likely dissociated before the molestation, which is why the wounds appeared during Phase Four. This client was unaware that this was happening to her wrists during EMDR. She made an adaptive shift seamlessly and reported at the end that she had never felt so good. "I have not felt this relaxed for decades." She was surprised by the wounds on her wrists but felt in a way her body was bearing witness to what she had endured as a child.

The T-EMDR therapist does not need to be afraid of disassociation or extreme body responses because we understand them and how to work with them. However, we must always practice within our scope and training, especially with more complex cases and conditions, so that we are prepared to support the client safely through the process.

Dr. Tinker expresses a "strong belief that traumatic reenactment should be open to scientific inquiry and formally researched" (B. Tinker, personal communication, May 21, 2025). Although we do not yet understand all the components and causes of traumatic reenactment, I know it is possible from my own lived experience, and I hope that my story can serve as a case study to our growing field of knowledge. The T-EMDR therapist also knows that it is possible and can support the client in understanding the depth of healing and resilience that it reflects.

In summary, Phase Four of EMDR is a highly active phase where the client processes distress related to the target through any of the six identified channels. This is also the point in processing when a client is most likely to experience somatization. As a T-EMDR therapist, you must be aware of these manifestations and, if the opportunity presents itself, invite the client to explore them further. The somatic bridge/floatback techniques can also be used in Phase Six (which will be discussed in Chapter 12), but caution must be exercised to ensure adequate time for the client to process any material that connects.

I hope that by reading this chapter, you will have a better understanding of how the body may express itself in Phase Four, the six channels of material, and how to work with somatization. By applying the principles of T-EMDR and attending to when the body speaks, we can resolve the unconscious distress that is feeding present symptoms. Or, as Dr. Shapiro puts it, we "help get this person to an actualized state" (Shapiro, 2003).

Chapter 8

Transformational EMDR Approach to the Query Response

What To Go With and Why

Dr. Andrew J. Dobo

Role induction before we begin

Role induction is a term used in psychotherapy to describe what typically happens at the beginning of treatment, which is the therapist's attempt to explain the treatment process. This explanation is essential and is a staple in any therapy; however, due to the unusual nature of EMDR, a clear and concise role induction must be stated more than once throughout the EMDR treatment. Those clients who have some familiarity with EMDR may need a less detailed explanation, while those who are unfamiliar with EMDR may need a more detailed explanation.

Transformational EMDR therapists explain the EMDR process, incorporating the psychoanalytic nature of EMDR into their explanation during the first meeting, as well as immediately before the first EMDR processing session.

This explanation is tailored to the client's specific needs. When working with a ten-year-old client, the explanation is designed so that the ten-year-old can understand. Often, therapists trained in other models come for EMDR therapy. Their role induction can be more detailed and even scientific if you are treating a therapist or anyone interested in the inner workings of psychological treatment. This explanation changes depending on the client; therefore, the therapist's depth and breadth of understanding of the EMDR model and the EMDR process are required. Their flexibility and intuitiveness, combined with their knowledge, ensure the client understands the process. As a result, the clients are more likely to trust it.

The eight phases of EMDR require two role inductions. The first role induction is a general and detailed explanation of EMDR, which is provided in the first session discussed in Chapter Four.

The second EMDR role induction is given immediately before Phase Four begins, that is, immediately before EMDR stimulation is initiated. Initially, these instructions can be comprehensive, but as the client becomes more familiar with their EMDR sessions, the instructions can distill to a few key reminders.

This role induction explains the client's role and what they can expect during EMDR processing. The therapist must remind the client that they can stop at any time. They are in control. Remind them of their safe place or any other resources you have in place. This way, you know that they know because you just told them that they can stop. This reminder that they, the client, is in control is comforting to the client, especially for trauma victims, who by definition experience loss of control. The client and the therapist both must understand that the client can stop at any time if they choose.

They are also told that it is best to push through the distress if possible. Repeating this instruction before each session ensures the client remembers these options during subsequent sessions. This way, the therapists will not be unsure and interrupt prematurely.

Transformational EMDR therapists remind the client that they will not experience anything that they have not already experienced and survived. EMDR does not create new trouble; it simply processes material from your life that is stored improperly. This improperly stored information is what causes problems in your life. They are encouraged to push through any distress because once they reach the other side of the experience, this material will never trouble them again. Never.

They are reminded that if they stop in the middle of an emotional discharge, we are just going to have to go to this same memory next session and start all over again; therefore, once the client is in this distress, it is best to push through so they can get to the end and never be troubled by these memories ever again. However, also remind them that if they need to stop, we can stop.

One of the essential elements of the BLS role induction is that Transformational EMDR therapists hear the psychoanalytic language. We emphasize and make sure the client understands what that means. The client is instructed not to edit their experiences at any given moment. The psyche speaks in images, metaphors, and symbols, so this instruction is essential for transformational work but really for all

EMDR work. This psychoanalytic component to the role induction may sound something like this:

> Every once in a while, I am going to stop and ask you what you are noticing. Please tell me what you are noticing at that moment. You do not need to summarize the last two minutes; just tell me what you are noticing at that very moment. Sometimes, our brains speak in metaphors and images. If you're thinking about a pumpkin, being on a school bus from second grade, or what you ate for dinner last Saturday, I want to hear about those things. Do not keep that kind of material from me. These things may seem silly or unimportant, but those bizarre things that come up often hold the key to everything, so please do not edit things that you may perceive as silly or unimportant. If it appears during this process, it is always important. Tell me what you are experiencing, no matter what it is (Dobo, 2018).

Transformational EMDR therapists typically include the following points as well.

They instruct the client to be a passive vessel. They are instructed not to try to make anything happen, nor are they to prevent anything from happening. Their job is to stay out of the way and ALLOW whatever is happening to happen.

The client is reminded that they do not need to understand what is happening, nor do they have to remember it. Their job is to allow whatever is happening to happen. It may make sense, or it may make absolutely no sense. It doesn't matter; just let whatever wants to happen to happen.

T-EMDR therapists remind them that if they begin to get upset, we do not stop. The client is reminded that the therapist does not stop to comfort them. The process works best if the emotion resolves itself naturally without interruption. They are reminded that they have a stop signal, but if at all possible, it is best to try to push through the distress.

The client is also told that if they start to experience something and, for some reason, they begin to push it back down because they "don't want to go there," they will just take that painful material home with them rather than letting it out and leaving it here in the therapist's office. They are reminded that whatever is processed here with me stays here. You are free of it if you allow it to be processed.

The client is told that whatever they prevent from processing, well, they get to take it home. That's okay if they are not ready to "go there." Hopefully, at some point, they will be prepared to get rid of the troubling memory. Remember, if there is something they do not want to share, they can just say, "I have an image or a memory" without revealing what it is.

We further explain the process using a movie metaphor as we begin.

> The image we decided to start with is like the first scene of a movie, and we do not know what the rest of the movie is going to be. You start with (the image we talked about), and you keep it in your mind's eye for a few seconds, along with the negative cognition and then just let go and allow your mind to free associate. Let it go wherever it wants to go. Sometimes, people say they see dozens of memories flash

before their eyes; that is fine. As best you can, allow whatever wants to happen to happen. Do not focus on one thing. Allow whatever is happening to happen (Dobo, 2018).

Internal experience

Phase Four is the phase where bilateral stimulation (BLS), also known as dual awareness stimulation (DAS), begins. It is the classic EMDR image of the "follow my hand with your eyes" moment. Once the stimulation begins, the EMDR process is underway. Phase Four is characterized by negative material. The proverbial saying is that we must go through hell to get to heaven.

Carl Rogers and Eugene Gendlin determined in their research that clients did not improve solely because of the therapist's technique or orientation. Clients change because they have an internal experience (Rogers, 1951; Gendlin, 1981). Without an internal experience, clients do not heal or change. The cliché "talk is cheap" is absolutely the case during EMDR therapy. The less you talk, the more powerful the result.

In recent years, clinicians have been trained to be wary of Phase Four of the client's authentic internal experience. I have heard endless stories from patients who encountered EMDR from clinicians who constantly interrupted just as an emotional discharge was about to happen. These are well-meaning but poorly trained clinicians who stop the process in the middle of an internal experience, which is the worst thing you can do.

It is important to note that the T-EMDR therapist never

times sets, never counts passes, but instead they closely observe the client while they wait, watch, and listen.

The critical point here is that the clinician cannot be afraid of what the client has to experience in Phase Four. Shapiro tells us that it is absolutely essential for the therapist to allow the client to process the material *exactly as it is currently stored.*

> Distortions are to be avoided. [Distortions are any intervention by the therapist that interrupts the process.] ... What does that mean? The pathology is based on the information **as it's currently stored** in the brain. Okay? The symptoms are coming up. The reactions are coming up from this information **the way it's currently stored**. The information is accessed **as it's currently stored**. When we bring together the image and cognition, and identify the emotion and physical sensations, we're placing the laser beams onto this, allowing us to access it in a controlled manner, **as it's currently stored**. But we need to make sure we're tracking it **as it's currently stored**. When we say, "What do you get now?" **it's coming up as it's currently stored.** And it's supposed to be processed **as it's currently stored** (Shapiro, 2003, bold mine).

The therapist does not change the expression in any way. Resourcing is not to be used because it alters the way the material is processed. Resources are only used if the client requests to stop or we have to stop because we are out of time, and they are dissociating. That is it!

I have had clients end up on the floor in my office wailing, and we do not stop. I have a video I share in my training with a client gagging and vomiting, and we do not stop. I processed a traumatic birth with a client who got on the floor as if she was giving birth, yelling and screaming. You guessed it. We do not stop. I share a video of clients who jerk and shake through all of Phase Four, then there is relief in Phase Five. These are extreme cases and rarely happen, but when they do, we do not stop. Recently, a colleague of mine sent pictures of a client who was bound around her wrists. He watched wounds appear on her wrist and skin open as if she were bound with rope. He was "freaked out," but he did not stop, and the client's relief was overwhelming after the session. The worst thing he could have done was to stop. We will discuss why this happens sometimes in later chapters.

When newly trained EMDR therapists are not told that these extreme responses can occur, they think the client is exceeding their window of tolerance when the client sheds a tear. They are not exceeding it. If they are present and know who they are, we do not stop. This is Shapiro's instruction that few seem to honor. Process the material as it is currently stored and don't interrupt unless the client is looping or blocked.

As I have said, Shapiro tells us we must allow the client to go where they need to go. I never got caught up in all the fashionable mindfulness and excessive resources because Shapiro described how detrimental this is to the EMDR process in that 2003 speech. As I was learning EMDR as a model, I remember saying to myself, "I do not want to be one of those therapists who are afraid of allowing the material to process as it is currently stored."

She said,

> We had a lot of trouble in the early days, where clients were getting training in cognitive behavior therapy and breathing skills. And so, as the middle of processing, they would start using their breathing technique, and the processing would stop. Because they just brought in another thing and not letting it stay there. The way it's currently stored needs to be available so that you're able to go down all of the associated channels that need to be processed. We've had clients, and you have them, and you're stabilizing them on benzodiazepines. We know that after you've processed, you need to go back and retarget, and you may find what was a zero is now at a five because the meds suppress the affect, which meant you're not getting to certain channels. That's why you have to go and process it again. **But the thing to keep in mind is that using guided visualization affirmations or whatever techniques you're using to suppress affect is also doing the same thing**. So if you find a need for doing this, you need to go back and do it in an undistorted manner (Shapiro, 2003).

I knew the excessive resourcing was unnecessary, even problematic, because I listened to Shapiro, and she was right. The sooner you do EMDR, the better. There is no need for excessive resourcing, because once you complete EMDR, the client's symptoms are alleviated, and they no longer require resources to manage them. The client feels content. They are okay in their own skin. They accept themselves and are at peace with themselves.

T-EMDR therapists spend twenty to thirty minutes on resourcing unless the client is fragile and needs extra time. Most people are stable enough to do EMDR in the third session. T-EMDR therapists use the first two sessions for preparation and start EMDR processing on the third session.

Query and set length

Transformational EMDR therapists understand that the query is supposed to habituate. The client should eventually not hear it, so it is not supposed to be interesting, and ideally, it should never change. This increases the likelihood of habituation. They will just notice the stimulation has stopped, and it is time to respond. Newly trained therapists often struggle with this. They feel like the query should not be redundant or boring, so they change it or make up phrases rather than simply asking, "What are you noticing?" When they change the query, sometimes the client will need clarification with a new query, saying something like, "What did you ask?" This is precisely what you do not want to happen. You just took them out of flow for nothing.

They say things like, "What's going on? What's happening? What are you experiencing?" Don't do this. The phrase "What are you noticing?"—it is the phase used in the research. The query is supposed to be boring so it does not interfere.

One of my trainees just could not say, "What are you noticing?" as instructed and invented the "What's going on?"

query. When I heard that query, the song "What's Going On" by Marvin Gaye started playing in my head. If you say, "What's going on?" that seems harmless enough, but if the client knows that song and you say that song title as your query, that song could start playing in the client's head. You just dramatically interfered with their processing.

Another acceptable query is, "What's coming up for you?" I prefer "What are you noticing?" It is shorter and habituates easily. "What is coming up for you?" is fine, but find the one you like and use it all the time. Habituation is the goal, not being interesting. Redundancy is the quality you are looking for.

There is a query that goes like this: "Okay, take a breath, clear it out. What is coming up for you?" T-EMDR therapists would never use this query because, as I have stated previously, the Transformational EMDR therapist attends to the client's breath. They time the end of the set to coincide with the client's exhalation. So they do not have to tell the client to take a breath because they just watched them take one.

Additionally, a T-EMDR therapist would never say "clear it out," because they do not want anything to clear out. They want to know what is going on with the client. There are times when a client is crying and has not taken a breath for a while. When we end that set, of course, we ask them to take a breath because they need a breath. There are exceptions to every rule. There is an appropriate time to ask the client to take a breath when they haven't taken one. You know this because you watch every breath.

To review, Transformational EMDR therapists know that the query should habituate. It is not supposed to change or be interesting. The T-EMDR therapist never tells the client to take a breath unless they have been upset and have not taken a breath in a while. Finally, the T-EMDR therapist coordinates the end of the set with an exhalation. In this way, the therapist is highly attuned to the client.

Hearing what no one else hears

Shapiro says we should never isolate material expressed in the query. We should not cherry-pick statements. We should say go with that after the client has finished sharing their thoughts. Later, she says that if there is a mixture of positive and negative material in a query response, we should always go with the negative material. In other words, she wants you to isolate material and cherry-pick. She contradicts herself, and this is one of the few places I disagree with her. Listening for what to go with is the art of EMDR.

The T-EMDR therapist listens with a discerning ear to every word the client says. They are also skilled at stopping excessive talking by the client that might interrupt the flow. I have discussed in great detail how the unconscious speaks to the therapist through the client in my previous book, *The Hero's Journey: Integrating Jungian Psychology and EMDR Therapy*. I will provide a few thoughts for you to consider as you listen to your clients, especially in Phase Four.

T-EMDR knows which materials are more durable than others. This is a basic premise of T-EMDR. Like I said earlier, the body is resistant to immediate resolution, as are emotions. Emotions tend to exist in more than one set. The unconscious speaks in metaphors, symbols, images, and common phrases like clichés. Unconscious material is like a dream; if you do not write the dream down immediately, it is gone forever. In Phase Four, images that are not from the three-dimensional world will be lost if you do not identify and go with them, just like a dream disappears immediately from your memory. For example:

> What are you noticing? "I'm locked in a glass box, and I feel really anxious right now. My chest is tight, and I want to scream because my father is such a selfish asshole."
>
> The response is, "Okay, notice you are locked in a glass box. Go with that."

This unconscious material is isolated because this image will disappear in the next set if the clinician goes with anything else. The tight chest will most likely be available for a somatic floatback in the next set or two if it is needed. Images like the glass box are priceless because they generalize throughout the client's life. How many times do you think this client wanted to scream or even did scream and no one heard her or cared what she had to say? Hence, the glass box. Going with the image is powerfully generalizable and travels to all relevant associated channels of the client's life. (I discuss identifying the language of the unconscious in my book *The Hero's Journey* in great detail.)

A T-EMDR therapist does not talk. They do not ask questions. Keeping the client in flow is the primary directive. Any gratuitous questions are a waste of time.

The T-EMDR therapist evaluates the material from the query response and instantly decides what statement is the most generalizable. This is to get the client in and out of Phase Four as fast as possible. The less talking and the more general, the more material gets covered in a short amount of time. For more detailed examples of what material is of high value and less value, and how to decide what to go with using expert skill, see my *Hero's Journey* book.

When to get a SUDS

There are only four reasons to get a SUDS, and sometimes you might not get a SUDS at all. The T-EMDR therapist never gets a SUDS if they can look at the client and make a pretty good guess about what the SUDS is at the moment for the client. If you can see they are upset, you don't have to ask them for a SUDS. You know it's between a seven and a nine. If you know or can guess, don't ask.

Never get a SUDS if the client is processing important material. Please do not interrupt the process by asking for a SUDS, which can disrupt flow. So, when do you get a SUDS?

1. If the client has been processing for fifteen or twenty minutes and there are no apparent signs of their level of distress. You should get a SUDS on the target to see where they are.
2. If the target has nothing to do with the session—for example, let's say you targeted an argument your client had with her husband as the target,

but all the material being processed in Phase Four is about her father and has little to do with the husband. Get a SUDS after fifteen or twenty minutes. Often, you will find the target of the husband is low, sometimes even zero. In this case, you can move to Phase Five anytime you feel is appropriate and install Phase Five because the target is no longer problematic. You may need to continue working on her issues with her father in subsequent sessions, even though Phase Four looks upsetting, because it is. The target is not distressing at all, so we are in Phase Five, even though it may not appear to be.

3. You get a SUDS after hearing two or three adaptive responses to the query. This usually signifies a move to Phase Five. This is the obvious time to get a SUDS.
4. The T-EMDR therapist knows that getting a SUDS can potentially break flow, so they look for places where there is an organic pause in processing rather than interrupting flow. Sometimes the client connects to a trauma that the therapist and the client have decided to wait on, but it connects in a session where some other target was used. To avoid going down this traumatic channel, the T-EMDR therapists use the SUDS to intentionally break flow and avoid overwhelming the client. So there are times when breaking flow is what is needed, and getting a

SUDS in these moments can accomplish that end.

There have been patient reports where their EMDR therapist got a SUDS after every third set. The patient never got to Phase Five and felt frustrated by the interruptions. I'm not sure where these ideas about getting a SUDS after three sets come from, but Shapiro tells us we should not have any preconceived notions about what should happen. This includes a predetermined number of sets and then get a SUDS. These arbitrary numbers have nothing to do with what is going on with the client. Just learn to wait, watch, and listen.

Chapter 9

Transformational EMDR's Antidote to Loops and Blocks

Interweaves, Extended Resources, and Problematic Parts

Dr. Andrew J. Dobo

As you have read in previous chapters and supported by Francine Shapiro in her 2003 keynote address, excessive resourcing is unnecessary in Phase Two, unless there are ecological factors in the session that require additional resourcing. A warning about excessive resourcing does not mean there is no place for parts work or ego state work during EMDR processing, as these interventions are essential when specific problems occur in Phase Four. Nor does it mean you should be reckless, starting EMDR prematurely. Still, Shapiro's point in her keynote was that most people do not need excessive resourcing, which is a serious problem today, because therapists are being taught to do exactly that, prepare and prepare some more.

This chapter describes how the T-EMDR therapist uses ego states, inner child, and the interweave design. These interventions are problem-solving strategies and are never used in Phase Two by the T-EMDR therapist because the therapist has no idea what the client will need or if they will need anything at all.

Meeting parts and establishing attachment figures sends the message that the therapist does not think you are strong enough to do this on your own. You might need your big brother as a resource, just as you always have, because you are the weak one.

No, we do not set up anything like that in advance. We follow Shapiro's instructions and do Phase Two as she instructed. Shapiro never once mentioned *attachment figures, parts work, or ego state work* in any of the three editions of *Eye Movement Desensitization and Reprocessing (EMDR) Therapy: Basic Principles, Protocols, and Procedures.* She definitely never recommended that any of these things be used in Phase Two.

The third edition was published in 2018. Shapiro was aware of all of these models. It is not by mistake that she omitted them. It is because they are not necessary. In fact, they interfere.

The T-EMDR therapist is aware and understands how to use parts, ego states, and attachment, but they are only used when and if they are needed. There is no advanced preparation for these things because it wastes time on things we may never need. We follow the client and always let the client tell us what they need when they need it. Not the other way around.

The T-EMDR therapist's goal is to help the client progress through Phases Four and Five as quickly as possible, thereby improving their quality of life. Resourcing takes fifteen to twenty minutes.

Shapiro states quite succinctly what is required in Phase Two:

> Preparation is just, can the client close down the disturbance in the session, and do they have something to allow them to close down the disturbance between sessions? If they can do that, you can process. You simply don't want them to be afraid of it, and you want to make sure they can stay present with you. Most clients need very little preparation because they are primarily intact (Shapiro, 2003).

These three sentences have gotten lost somewhere along the way as mindfulness and other models invaded EMDR. It has become fashionable for therapists to have clients establish an attachment figure in Phase Two or to talk to a part that the therapist suggested they need to reconcile. This is set up by asking if the client has a person in their life they might bring into problematic scenes. Some attachment trainings ask the trainee to establish a nurturer, protector, or wisdom figure that the client can establish in Phase Two before starting any EMDR. The client is asked to have a conversation with each figure to develop them.

The reason T-EMDR therapists never do this in Phase Two is twofold. First, the therapist has undue influence—their words have power. By informing the client that they may need assistance and asking who might help them, you're essentially telling them what they have likely heard their entire life. "You just aren't strong enough to do this on your own." "You are going to need help, just like you have always needed help, so let's get you that help before we start."

By suggesting this in Phase Two, the therapist conveys to the client that their therapist is just like everyone else. The therapist's implicit message is that they do not believe the client can do this on their own, either.

The second reason is that the therapist has no idea what the client will need, if anything. Again, they are not following the client; they are leading.

T-EMDR therapists always strive to empower their clients. From the very first meeting, the goal is to create an empowered, grounded, and authentic individual. The therapist is aware of all of these interventions and resources but will only use them if the client requires them.

Extended resourcing in Phase Four

The T-EMDR therapist relies on the following three common extended resourcing strategies frequently. The hallmark characteristic of all these strategies is that the client remains in the EMDR stimulation as long as necessary to change the narrative using their imagination. There is no query during the Inner Child extended resource.

Suppose we start with an interweave because the client is looping in a childhood memory of being trapped with their perpetrator in their childhood home, and the interweave did not work. In that case, we move to a more advanced intervention called the Inner Child Extended Resource.

In keeping with our follow-the-client-directive and psychoanalytic hands-off approach, our instructions are vague and straightforward because we do not know what the client needs to change the narrative. The directive is as follows:

You always ask permission. You ask the client if they are able, as their adult self, to go back in the scene and

1. Bring your child-self to safety.
2. Give her what she needed at the time that she did not get.
3. Take as much time as you need. The stimulation will not stop until you say you are finished or if you need help.

Usually, with adults, the adult self is strong enough, and it is preferred because it empowers the client. If the adult self is not enough, or if you are working with a child, you can offer additional resources, such as the attachment figures we mentioned earlier.

The T-EMDR therapist never suggests an attachment figure or anything else. The first thing the therapist asks is, "Is there someone you might bring into the scene with you to make you feel safe?"

Remember, the answer is always within the client, not with you or some book you read. Any opportunity you have to put the responsibility on the client, use it.

Once this intervention is complete, there is often a shift to Phase Five. It is often a good time to get a SUDS on the original target after this extended resource.

They can bring someone into the scene for strength if needed.

- It can be anyone, whether real or fictional.
- It can be the person as an adult who stands up to the childhood bully.
- It can be a strong family member.
- It can be you, the therapist.
- It can be the police or some made-up warriors.
- Kids like superheroes. It can be any of these.
- Some people bring in religious figures, such as Jesus, Buddha, or other revered figures.
- A nurturer in their life.
- A protector, real or imagined.
- A wisdom figure.

It is entirely up to them.

Grief and loss extended resourcing

An extended active imagination strategy for grief and loss: The client can use their imagination to speak to a deceased loved one if they choose. This intervention is not set up in advance, but it is suggested in Phase Four.

If it seems like the client might like to speak to the deceased person, you can offer this extended resource. It is done in much the same way as the previous extended resource. The client can take as much time as they want. Stimulation will continue until they have completed the conversation with the loved one. This process can sometimes take ten or fifteen minutes or more, as imagined. This process can be highly emotional and healing.

Sometimes the session ends when the client completes

this conversation with the deceased person. Use your judgment whether to discontinue or not. Often, the client experiences such relief that it's a good time to stop.

Setting up the grief and loss extended resource

You ask the client if they would like to speak to the deceased person. Always ask permission, because not everyone wants to speak to the loved one.

If they say yes, then you ask, "Can you imagine a place where you can talk?" Once they have their place, then you continue with the final instruction:

1. I want you to close your eyes and go and have that conversation with him/her.
2. Take all the time you need. I will not stop the stimulation. Please let me know when you are finished.

That's it. Continue tracking nonverbal cues. This can often be an emotional experience, so it's a good idea to have tissues available before you start. Once they finish this process, the session may end immediately. The relief is so profound, and it is often best to let them leave with the peace they found in this intervention. Again, use your judgment. You may want to continue with the phases but allow yourself and the client to call it quits if that seems to be the wisest course of action.

Reconciling with the inner child and integrating the inner child

Reconciling with the inner child can be seen as parts work or ego state work. The strategies below are the only "parts work" that the T-EMDR therapist typically uses. These are powerful interventions and are seen as staples of the standard protocol.

When one encounters a problematic part, manifested in a problematic behavior, the intervention is always the same. The client must thank the part and then convince the part that the behavior they are still engaging in was effective as a child but no longer works as an adult. The client must find a way, using their imagination with bilateral stimulation, to convince the child to let go of the childlike behavior.

Again, the instructions are vague because the therapist has no idea what the inner child needs to hear to change the behavior. Only the client's inner self knows the answer, so the instructions are as follows:

1. Go into the scene and thank the younger you. Thank the child for being invisible and passive to be safe. So thank the child for getting us to this point in our life safely.
2. Then convince the child that we have other ways to be safe as adults. We no longer have to be quiet or invisible to be safe. It is okay to say what you want and need.

Reconciling with the inner child

The insidious nature of the maladaptive behavior as an adult, like being a doormat, is that being passive makes a lot of sense if your father is a raging, violent alcoholic. Hiding in your room or running to a friend's house at the first hint of emotion makes perfect sense for a kid, but this no longer works as an adult. Just doing what you are told, not standing up for yourself, and keeping quiet to avoid being beaten is a smart thing for a kid to do.

The problem occurs when, as an adult, the person continues to use these smart child strategies into adulthood, when they stop working. If you do not speak up for yourself as an adult, you will be taken advantage of in all areas of your life. These clients live their lives from an *I don't matter* position. I don't matter; everyone else does. Alcohol mattered to my dad; I did not matter.

With all *I don't matter* clients, child ego state resists the new way, the new perspective of *I do matter*. The problematic child part often says, "We're not going to speak up now. The last time we spoke up, we got beaten so bad we almost died. No, thank you. I'll take being taken advantage of over death anytime."

It is up to the client to find a way to convince the child ego state. And the client always finds the answer if you, as the therapist, have them in the state of flow. The T-EMDR therapist knows they do not know the answer. They know the client must discover the answer within themselves.

The interweave

An interweave is required for several different reasons, but perhaps the most common reason is that the AIP model breaks down, causing the PAST to be present in the session. Shapiro tells us, "Because processing means the client will go where they need to go, and are you ready to let them do that? There's the dual awareness for them of one foot in the past and one foot in the present" (Shapiro, 2003). Interweaves are used because both feet are stuck in the past, and they cannot free themselves from the past memory in which they are presently stuck. We call this a loop.

How do we solve this problem? We simply ask a question that you know the answer to. This question will take the client out of the past and bring them safely into the present. Once they answer the question, immediately say, "Go with that."

It is essential to respond quickly with "go with that" once you hear what you wanted them to say. It is usually simply yes or no. You instantly say, "Go with that..." If you pause, it gives them time to retreat to a negative thought.

You sometimes have to be very quick with the "go with that" statement. Once the client says what you want to hear, you immediately and enthusiastically say, "Go with that." Do not delay because you want to head off the "but" that could take them back to the negative material. There is no guarantee that they won't go back to the negative, but you enhance the chance of opening the adaptive channel by heading off the "but."

Proper design and deployment of the interweave

Interweaves are to be quick, concise, and maintain flow. You should know what interweave you will need before you start Phase Four. The interweave is predictable. So be prepared for it, but you may not need it. Do not rush in. It is best if the client gets there independently. Their internal experience is at stake, so give them time to figure it out on their own, but if they struggle, help them with a quick and concise interweave. The interweave is not a discussion or an insight. It is a quick question that you know the answer to.

For example, if you have a client whose negative cognition is *I don't matter*, the T-EMDR therapist knows this client might go down some predictable rabbit hole where they are saying things like, "No one ever cared about me. All my dad ever cared about was my brother and baseball. My mom loved alcohol, not me." "I got blamed for everything. My brother never got blamed for anything, and he was nothing but trouble." These statements may all be factual. The T-EMDR therapist understands they need to know who they have now or had as a kid as a support person. Someone they mattered to—the person who is the antidote to this negative material.

T-EMDR therapists always want to know about the client's grandparents or any other person who cared about them in the past or still cares about them now. It is often the grandmother, so if I know this, Grandma is the interweave I have prepared in my mind. If they have a good marriage and a good relationship with their kids, these relationships can be used in an interweave.

As the client loops in these thoughts,

"No one cared. No one loved me. People wouldn't care if I lived or died."

I would say as the interweave, "Didn't you say your grandmother loved you?"

"Yes, my grandmother loved me." Immediately say, "Go with that ..." after that statement. Often, we are concerned about the words of the interweave as we should be, but also the timing of your response to the client's words is essential. Do not hesitate, because you want to prevent the client from saying "but." You want to head off the "but": "Yes, my grandmother loved me, **but** that was a long time ago. No one cares about me now." You say "go with that" after they say, "Yes, my grandmother loved me." Immediately say, *Go with that.*

It is essential to interrupt as soon as you hear the positive statement you want to hear, thus preventing the negative material from interfering. It is crucial to repeat the positive response with encouragement in your voice to reinforce the positive response to the interweave and soften the interruption.

Common Phase Four situations that require interweaves

This is not a comprehensive list of interweaves. These are common ones, but interweaves often require creativity on the therapist's part. We will address those later.

Some examples are below:

Interweave for adults who had a learning disability as a child

If you have a client who had a learning disability and struggled in school but has a master's degree now, they often find themselves weeping about the struggles in their past that can cause a loop that traps them in their past. The memories are of parents yelling at them while they were doing their homework, calling them stupid, and comparing them to other kids, or being embarrassed in the classroom because they were poor readers or struggled to understand math.

It is common for people with this background to have multiple college degrees. This is in the service of proving to themselves and the world that they are not stupid and that they are good enough. You want to explore their success at work or in their life, which demonstrates they are not stupid, and use these successes as material for the interweave.

Loop: The client is crying. "My dad is just yelling at me because I didn't understand. For years, I endured that kitchen table rant about being stupid."

The interweave is:
"Don't you have a master's degree?"
"Yes."
"Go with that."

This question immediately brings them to the present, and they realize they are not stupid, nor are they the child who felt stupid as a kid anymore. Usually, this interweaving causes them to laugh at how silly it was to be crying about their past. It's not foolish at all. This emotional pain is being processed as it is presently stored, which is what Shapiro tells us to do. As a child, they were trapped. There was no way out for years, so being trapped in this loop makes perfect sense and is predictable to the T-EMDR therapist. As you can see, nothing too mysterious, just a question you know the answer to that brings the client from the past to their present reality.

Example interweave for car accident victims who eventually ended up being okay

Sometimes, people get into car accidents and are unsure how they managed to get out of the car. They might have been unconscious, so they do not have that memory. As long as you know everyone ended up being okay, when they loop and say something like, "I can't get out. I'm trapped in the car. I can't get out":

The interweave is:
"But everyone is okay now, right?"
"Yes, everyone is okay."
"Okay, go with that."

If you know the client's wife met the client at the hospital, the interweave might be,

"Didn't you say your wife was there holding your hand when you arrived at the hospital?"
"Oh, yeah, that's right."

"Okay, go with that memory of her holding your hand."

Common interweave for suicidal ideation

Most clients who are depressed have suicidal ideation. They do not have an intent or a plan, but they are in psychological pain. They wish they could die in their sleep but have no intent on killing themselves. They often say things like, "I just wish I would not wake up in the morning or that I would get cancer and die." Thoughts like that are often part of depression. The T-EMDR therapist, while assessing suicide, notes the reasons why the client would never kill themselves. Common reasons are, "I would never do that to my wife or kids; I would never abandon them like that." Some people are religious and say things like, "I would never kill myself. It is against my religion, and it is a sin against God." Sometimes people love their pets and would not kill themselves because they don't want their pet to be abandoned. Whatever reason they give is material for an interweave. During Phase Four, these clients will sometimes say things like,

Loop: "I wish I were dead; no one cares if I stay around."
Interweave: "Didn't you say you would never kill yourself because you love your family?
"Oh yeah, I'd never kill myself. I'd never do that to my family."
"Okay, go with that."

The therapist does a thorough history to gather the necessary information to design an effective interweave based on the client's problem, even suicidal ideation—or especially suicidal ideation.

Example interweave for child abuse

Sometimes, in a situation where a child was trapped by a perpetrator who lived with them, like a stepdad or brother, the client loops in a childhood situation. They will often turn to you and say, "I'm trapped. I can't get out."

The interweave is:
"You're safe now, right?"
"Yes, I am."
"Okay, go with that."
or
"You were strong and survived all of that. Right?"
"Yes, I am, and I did."
"Okay, go with that."

This situation sometimes requires more than an interweave. Extended resourcing is often necessary, but it is worth trying the interweave first.

Sometimes the interweave is something you may have already said to the client. Interweaves are not complicated or mysterious. The problem is that your client is stuck in the past, and you ask them a question that will bring them to the present reality.

Please note that these interweaves are not the only ones

to use in the examples, although these exact interweaves are frequently used. They should give you an idea of how to predict what interventions you may need based on the client's history. Interweaves from the therapists' inner genius that occurred while they were in flow. Interweaves that you will not find in any books. This is where your units of human achievement come in, as well as your ability to enter flow as the therapist.

Ryan's Chinese medicine interweave gave a client permission to cry. A man who never cried, not even at his wife's funeral. Serena's Bronx, New York, Italian "I can't take another minute of this avoidance from this client" interweaves. Serena's Bronx cut-the-bullshit interweave opened a floodgate of tears for the client. The "go with the pumpkin" interweave or the "Christmas elf" conversation interweave that changed everything in the sessions. The genius that the EMDR therapist possesses is not always found in EMDR books, but you have to start there.

To review, the problem-solving solutions for the T-EMDR therapist are as follows:

1. The interweave, where you ask a question that you know the answer to, brings the client out of the past and into the present. This question is quick to ensure we keep the client in flow. You quickly say, "Go with that" to prevent the client from getting to the "but."
2. Extended resource, which occurs when you bring in the adult self or another figure to change the narrative in a scene where the client escapes the

perpetrator. The adult self goes in, takes the child to safety, and gives the child what they did not get as a child.

3. Talking to the deceased person. You ask if the client would like to speak to the deceased person. If yes, you ask them where they might have that conversation. Once the place is established, tell them to take as much time as they want. Turn the stimulation on and only stop it when they are finished.
4. Integrating the inner child is when the adult self must make peace with the child ego state. This is done by thanking the child for engaging in the adaptive behavior as a child. Then convince the child part to let go of the behavior because, as an adult, it is maladaptive and no longer works. The client has to do the convincing.

Remember, none of these interventions are established in advance with the client. They are all utilized in Phase Four, only if needed.

Chapter 10

The Grave Harm of Excessive Resourcing, Gratuitous Integration, and Fear of Abreactions

Delaying or Interrupting EMDR Unnecessarily Harms the Client

Dr. Andrew J. Dobo

Melinda discussed the harm of excessive resource allocation in Chapter Five. Because it is a significant problem in today's EMDR ecosystem, it is necessary to provide specific examples of why this is a problem and how it actually harms clients by sharing three case studies. It is essential to reiterate the extent of the harm done by delaying EMDR to add other models or add unnecessary and excessive resourcing.

We might want to consider Leidy Klotz, the author of *Subtract,* who explains how taking away from a system can make it stronger and adding to a system often weakens the system. He quotes Antoine de Saint-Exupery, the author of *The Little Prince,* who observed, "Perfection is achieved, not when there is nothing more to add, but when there is nothing left to take away." Klotz also discusses Kurt Koffka's idea that the whole of a system can be greater than the sum of its parts, but unnecessarily adding can make the opposite true. The whole can be less than the sum of its parts, and sadly, in many pockets of EMDR training and practice, that is where we are.

Adding to a system that often diminishes its overall performance.

T-EMDR therapists eliminate as much as possible from the EMDR process. They adhere to the standard protocol, refraining from conversation or questioning unless a problem arises. The only question they ask is, "What are you noticing?" It may seem like we are beating a dead horse here, but let's look at a few cases.

Below are three examples of unnecessary delays that harmed clients, but I have literally dozens of similar examples that I hear whenever I teach a training. Someone inevitably comes up to me and tells me a horror story about their EMDR treatment experience.

Francine Shapiro was not a fan of excessive resourcing and mindfulness practices that delayed the use of EMDR therapy. When I heard her 2002 speech, I was not sure why she was so angry about a little extra relaxation before starting. She saw the danger, and now it is a plague across the EMDR ecosystem.

Below are three examples that caused harm when a clinician set up unnecessary attachment figures, gathering committee or meeting parts in advance, rather than following the client, adhering to standard protocol, and following Francine Shapiro.

A trainee of mine had a horrific, traumatic birth experience of her first child; she almost died, and she thought her child died as part of the experience. Subsequently, she was having flashbacks all day long, to the point that seeing her happy, healthy baby who was safely at home with her was causing flashbacks for this new mom. It was a powerfully distressing situation. She is a trained EMDR therapist, trained by me.

She sought out an "EMDR therapist." This therapist would not start EMDR with her until she was able to talk to her "wisdom figure." My trainee was not able to speak to a wisdom figure; she did not want to talk to a wisdom figure, but her therapist insisted that she was not ready for EMDR until she could speak to this wisdom figure. This prerequisite is based on nothing. No research on the planet says you cannot start EMDR until you speak to your wisdom figure, but here we are. There is no scientific literature that requires talking to someone in your imagination before initiating EMDR. Yet, she was presented with this bizarre request. A request that is harming the client by withholding treatment.

My trainee, let's call her Sarah to protect her privacy, wanted EMDR, not a chat with an imagined entity. After three sessions of not doing EMDR, she contacted me in desperation. I met with her once. She already had a resource —a safe place—because she is a trained EMDR therapist, and everyone who trains with me knows all eight phases of EMDR, and they all have their own safe place. We conducted an emotionally charged virtual EMDR session. After this sole EMDR session, she no longer had flashbacks. She was able to enjoy her baby's first Christmas. That is the only session she needed. After one sixty-minute session, she regained her life, enjoying her new baby and her baby's first Christmas. This upfront unnecessary preparation clearly was harmful.

T-EMDR therapists know that a single-episode event can be resolved immediately, typically with a single resource: a safe place. I've treated about ten couples who lost a child. I do EMDR during the second session, which is sometimes the day after the intake, because they are in such pain. Can you imagine if I said to a parent whose child died, "First, you have to talk to your wisdom figure"?

Second, a trainee who attended my training shared her experience with EMDR. She did not have a big *T* trauma, just some childhood things that bothered her, and she wanted to work on them. Transformational EMDR therapists typically begin EMDR in session three with individuals like this, almost without exception. Most likely, she would complete the work in a few sessions. Her therapist insisted that she meet all of her parts. She had to talk to her avoidant part, her inner critic part, her escapist part, and on and on. She did this for a month before they even talked about EMDR. She said she got more out of one practice session as a client at our training than she ever did from seeing her EMDR therapist the past two months. The issue is that the therapist has no idea which part, if any, is a problem. They are guessing. Phase Four shows if and what part is a problem, not the therapist's gratuitous guess.

A client was molested by her grandfather when she was five. Common sense tells the all-knowing therapist she will need a protector. The T-EMDR therapist makes no such assumption. We follow the client. We wait until Phase Four shows us what is needed, if anything.

At first, the client was able to go into the scene alone but stopped and said, "I need Miss Kay Kay!" The therapist had no idea who Miss Kay Kay was but asked, "Can you bring Miss Kay Kay in?" The client said yes and continued, and in minutes, she was able to resolve this trauma with Miss Kay Kay. Miss Kay Kay was not a protector. She was her childhood nanny, whom she loved and who loved her in return. She was her nurturer. So, this idea that the therapist knows is dangerous and actually arrogant. EMDR works best when the therapist starts with, "I don't know."

Finally, I could go on and on about the cases that people complain to me about. The third troubling case was a woman who went to see an EMDR therapist here, somewhere in Florida. In the middle of processing, her eye started to twitch, a common occurrence in Phase Four. This twitching apparently horrified the therapist. The therapist stopped and told this client EMDR was not appropriate for her and sent her on her way with a twitching eye. The eye would not stop twitching. It twitched for a week. She was ready to go to the emergency room. They would not have a clue in the emergency room. They would probably order tests and give her drugs. Fortunately, she called one of my colleagues whom I trained. He asked a few questions and did three more sets of EMDR on the twitching. The twitching stopped, and there was a positive shift into Phase Five. This all took about fifteen minutes. So we go from excessive resourcing to no resourcing at all.

Like I said, open Shapiro's *Basic Principles, Protocols, and Procedures* book and search "meet your parts," the IFS of Internal Family Systems thing, and see what she says about it. You guessed it. It is never mentioned. Shapiro spends two and a half pages discussing resourcing in her text—that is it! As I mentioned, she was not a fan of extra resourcing because she believed excessive resourcing was a waste of time. If the client can calm themselves with a safe place, then we are ready to start.

All this talking to parts, having a gathering committee, and attachment figures before we begin, delays getting to the work that heals and reduces or eliminates distress, and that is EMDR standard protocol, administered as Shapiro and her thirty years of research instruct. All of these unnecessary additions to EMDR are doing precisely what Shapiro warned against. They delay processing, which is where the healing occurs. She lamented the excessive resourcing in 2003, and it has gotten far worse today. She said,

> We have had an upsurge in clients calling the institute over the past year saying, "I'm really confused. I've been doing EMDR for weeks or months. I love my clinician, we have a great rapport, and I feel great at the end of every session, but when I go home, my issues are still there. I'm just not getting any better, and I read this book, and it doesn't sound like what they're doing is EMDR." They say, "Well, did you speak to the therapist?" And I said, yeah, preparation is great. Everybody doesn't need a lot of preparation. You know that's the bottom line because the preparation isn't the processing (Shapiro, 2003).

If your client reads the EMDR book, they will find nothing about IFS, nothing about polyvagal, and nothing about gathering committees or talking to a wisdom figure. As I mentioned, Shapiro devotes only two and a half pages of the 568-page book to the preparation phase. That is not by accident or because she was unaware of all these other practices infiltrating her model. She knew it, warned us about it, but few people heeded this warning. Too many people are fixing things that are not broken. If you have one resource that works, you can and must begin. I spent almost a thirty-year EMDR career using only a safe place and some breathing skills. That is it.

Please do not think I am suggesting clinicians become careless or cavalier. There are times when patients need a comprehensive psychological evaluation. They need multiple psychological assessments because they are so damaged. Military population with severe PTSD may be inpatient and require a great deal of time and a considerable amount of evaluation, both psychological and psychiatric. Know your patient.

I am not suggesting you should not learn IFS, polyvagal, or any other model that interests you. Learn everything you can. What I am saying is that all the knowledge you possess should be used when there is a problem during EMDR but not preemptively. For example, you should not try this new technique on an unsuspecting client who wants EMDR just because you took a course last weekend and you want to try out this new technique. That is the exact opposite of client-centered.

In private practice or outpatients, most of the time, as Shapiro states, patients are well enough put together to start EMDR. If they have a job, a family, coach soccer, drive, and have a stable life, it is unlikely that you need to start administering excessive psychological testing. As Shapiro mentioned, if they can calm themselves with a resource, you can start using EMDR.

Let us consider the wisdom of Lao Tzu. "To attain knowledge, add things every day. To attain wisdom, subtract things every day" (Klotz, 2021). One must attain knowledge. Education, study, and experience are all in the service of gaining knowledge, but then there is a point where you understand what is needed and when it is needed, and what is not needed. So keep learning; just be careful when you add. It is pretty simple with EMDR: If there is no problem, there is nothing to add. Just keep the client in flow and stay out of the way.

The fear of the abreaction

There are few things that are more harmful to a client than a therapist who is afraid to allow the material to process as it is currently stored. Especially when they are in the middle of a powerful abreaction. This is really no time to stop. That means the therapist must have the ability to sit quietly while the client wails, shakes, twitches, and screams. Fearful clinicians have an excuse to shut processing down prematurely because they can say, "The client is exceeding their window of tolerance."

When Daniel Siegel introduced the idea of the window of tolerance, I doubt he thought it would be used to shut down processing prematurely because of the therapists' fear, but here we are. The T-EMDR therapist considers the window of tolerance being exceeded if the client dissociates to the level of not being present or if the client asks to stop. That is it. As you have heard in previous chapters, clients vomit, and we continue. Clients slide off the chair into a fetal position, holding the tappers, and we do not stop. Clients develop wounds and bruises right before our eyes, and we do not stop. The worst thing you could do to a client is interrupt them in the middle of such abreactions because all that means is you are going to ask them to do this all over again at the next session because you could not tolerate it in the present session.

Shapiro tells us we must allow the material to be processed as it is currently stored.

> The reactions are coming up from this information the way it's currently stored. The information is accessed as it's currently stored. When we bring together the image and cognition, and identify the emotion and physical sensations, we're placing the laser beams onto this, allowing us to access it in a controlled manner, as it's currently stored.
>
> But we need to make sure we're tracking it as it's currently stored. When we say, what do you get now? It's coming up as it's currently stored. And it's supposed to be processed as it's currently stored (Shapiro, 2003).

If the client is brave enough to fall to the floor and process, and you are not brave enough to let them, then, as Shapiro suggests, you need to work on your own stuff.

> It's very important who you are and what ... you need to do to feel present and not afraid of what the person is going to be experiencing. Are you all right with what they need to experience, or are you going to say to them, "No, you don't have to feel that right now; no, it's okay"? Just think,

everyone has different tolerance levels, affect tolerance levels. What's yours?

If you see a client feeling their disturbance, do you have the sense it's dangerous for them? Are you telling your client, "Don't feel; be afraid of your feelings"? Are you giving them the same messages that they got early on: "Don't feel it. Don't express it. The other person will run away. The other person will think it's shameful. I'll disintegrate." All those messages that are in there. Have you cleaned them out of your system? Because processing means the client will go where they need to go, and are you ready to let them do that? There's the dual awareness for them of one foot in the past and one foot in the present, noticing it as it emerges (Shapiro, 2003).

Linda Khmelnytska recently had a session that she describes below. One of the reasons I chose Linda to participate in this book is because of her fearlessness during EMDR sessions. I have watched videos of her modeling a complete sense of calm in the midst of high emotion. This description of one of her recent cases demonstrates the need for such fearlessness during EMDR sessions.

My client, thirty-eight years old, started by saying something "really stupid" had happened. I love when clients start like that because it usually turns out to be profound. The target was my client giving a massage session when her client told her she didn't like what she was doing. Instead of hearing it as feedback, my client said her whole being curled into a ball, and she felt terrified.

The NC started as "I'm doing something wrong," which we funneled down to "I'm going to be punished," and finally landed on "I am bad." Phase Four was intense, and she was processing beautifully. Then, suddenly, she teared up. Her face turned red, then deep purple as I realized she wasn't breathing for more than a minute. She started grinding her teeth, and within seconds, she let out a scream that was indescribable. She kept screaming like that for almost five minutes—four minutes, fifty-three seconds, to be exact.

The sound was so raw and primal that the therapists in the offices next to me stopped their sessions. Honestly, I got scared not because I didn't know what to do because she was so animated and the energy was violent. The only way I can describe that scream is that it sounded like she was stabbing someone she deeply loved. I know, it's a weird comparison.

I heard Dr. Dobo's voice in my head: "It has a beginning, a middle, and an end." So I stayed still. And sure enough, at 4:53, it ended. She shifted to Phase Five with "I'm not bad."

When the session was over, the other two therapists who were trained by Dr. Dobo came into my office, eyes wide, silent. We debriefed, and it turned into such a powerful conversation about what happens when our own fear shows up in the room and how important it is not to let that fear run the session.

It was one of those sessions that leaves you in awe of EMDR and the human psyche.

After that scream, something sacred happened. She

told me she spent the evening with her declining father—no overthinking, no analyzing, no guarding. She just sat with him, laughed at his stories, and soaked him in. Then she said, "For the first time in thirty-eight years, I wasn't trying to survive him. I was just with him."

Chapter 11

Transformational EMDR Approach to Phase Five

The Adaptive Shift Is More Than a Low SUDS

Dr. Andrew J. Dobo

Perhaps the transition between Phases Four and Five is the most crucial phase. This is the part of the session where beginners lose control of the session. Once a client demonstrates an adaptive shift, the T-EMDR clinician is on alert because they know the session may be coming to a close.

When the clinician hears or sees an adaptive shift, the therapist asks the client to go with the adaptive material but shortens the set and checks in again to see if the shift remains positive. If the patient makes another positive statement, the clinician can decide to tell the client to go with that, the new positive statement, or they can install the positive statement that they prepared in Phase Three and pair it with the negative image and the positive thought.

The clinician must use their judgment to determine how many sets to allow before the installation. The key factor is the content of the material. If the client is saying incredibly empowering statements, one might allow that to continue for a couple of sets, to reinforce those robust statements before the installation. If the statements are not as provocative, one can move to the installation, which is the official start of Phase Five. The T-EMDR therapist knows to keep this set short to reduce the likelihood of a shift backward to troubling material. If the material stays positive after imposing the negative image on the Phase Five material, the therapist can do a few more short sets and move to Phase Six, the body scan. This is basically how to handle Phase Five. Especially if one is working with a therapeutic hour, because time is of the essence, if a client has moved into the adaptive place, we want to send them home there.

There is a troubling, even damaging practice that clinicians are engaging in. They are rigidly insisting that Phase Five only begins when the SUDS scale (Subjective Units of Distress scale) is zero or one. This rigid practice has harmed more clients and caused more mental distress for clients than almost any other practice I have witnessed. Not only does it harm the client, but clinicians I have talked to report that they stopped using EMDR because in the session, clients shift to an adaptive way of thinking, but their SUDS is only a three so they rigidly follow the Phase Five rule that the SUDS must be a zero or one. So they take the client back to the negative image and negative thought. Soon the client finds themselves in the midst of new distressing material. Now, time is up, the session is ending, and they are forced to use a resource, sending the client away in distress. This pattern has caused well-meaning therapists to stop using EMDR. It has stopped the client from wanting to use EMDR. Rigid thinking in general, but specifically with the SUDS, is harmful to the client, the therapist, and the reputation of EMDR therapy. Remember Kurt Lewin: The best way to change behavior is to reduce limiting forces. There is nothing more restraining to this system we call EMDR than insisting on a SUDS of zero-one and ignoring everything else that is happening in the session.

Shapiro never said Phase Five must have a zero-one SUDS, or you are not in Phase Five. She NEVER said this. Here is what she said. I will admit it is a poorly written sentence, but she had no idea how this single sentence's misinterpretation would be seen as a religious law.

> After initial reprocessing has been achieved, with the accessed target emerging at no greater than a SUDS rating of 0-1 (unless otherwise ecologically appropriate; e. g., "I'm sorry he died") (Shapiro, 2018).

So, what does "unless otherwise ecologically appropriate" mean? It means, are there any other factors that would demonstrate we are in Phase Five besides a zero-one SUDS? Phase Five is not a SUDS rating; it is a state of mind. Factors to consider:

1. The patient might be a terrible self-reporter of SUDS. So the SUDS is almost completely unreliable, for example. The client was crying and shaking at the beginning of the session. We started at a SUDS of nine, and Phase Four was grueling. It resolved itself. The client is breathing calmly, relaxed with no tears, saying adaptive thoughts. When asked what her SUDS felt like

now, she says eight. Looking at other ecological factors other than the SUDS, the clinician observes SUDS of two. The clinician is permitted to use their experience, skill, and observation talent to make their determination about the SUDS and what phase the client is in. This client is clearly in Phase Five.

2. Sometimes a client will not provide an accurate SUDS because they cannot believe that the memory that has haunted them for twenty years is gone in twenty minutes of EMDR. They cannot imagine that such a thing is possible, so they will not give you an accurate SUDS because they cannot believe it.
3. The target may be a deceased loved one. With clients who lost a loved one, they do not want a SUDS of zero or one. They want relief, but they also want to feel sad, just not overwhelming, paralyzing grief. A SUDS of three or four should be the target for the death of a loved one, never zero.

If one rigidly insists on a zero-one SUDS, with this client, who will always say eight no matter what is going on with them, you will never get to Phase Five. If this is the only piece of data one uses to determine Phase Five, you will never get to Phase Five with this client. Ironically, this client is in Phase Five. She is saying and feeling positive, but because her SUDS is eight, the rigid-thinking therapist takes the client back to Phase Four. "Let's go back to the negative image and the negative thought and keep going." In essence, taking the client backward to the negative material at the end of the session, even though they are in Phase Five.

The client is telling the therapist that the session is ending with the adaptive shift. But because the SUDS is high, this reality is ignored by the rigid-thinking therapist, so the client is often sent home with a session that is not closed appropriately for no other reason than the therapist does not follow the client or recognize Phase Five beyond a SUDS scale. T-EMDR therapists take data from a variety of sources to determine Phase Five, like what the client is saying and showing in their body and breathing—how the original target seems to affect them, no matter what the SUDS self-report is. They also evaluate the SUDS self-report through the lens of their experience and skill.

The art of managing Phase Five

Shapiro tells us that you should never cherry-pick material from a query response. Then she contradicts this statement. She also says that if a response contains positive and negative material, you should always go with the negative. I guess cherry-pick the negative from the positive. This rule she expresses here is not always true. It depends.

If I just started a session and I am on the third set, the response includes negative and positive material. I will go with the negative material, because it is too early in the session to be in Phase Five. Here, I agree with Shapiro's statement. If, however, it is the ninth or tenth set and I am running out of time in the session, and a query response contains both negative and positive material, I isolate the positive material, shorten the set, and attempt to open the adaptive channel to Phase Five. If time is not an issue, I will continue with the negative material; however, these days, time is often an issue, and I want the client to leave in Phase Five so the adaptive material can continue processing after they leave the session.

Remember, Phase Five is a state of mind, not a client self-report of the SUDS. Do not be afraid to trust your intuition, judgment, and observation skills. Always attune to the client. They will tell you where you are without uttering a word. Sometimes the only thing that is required is for you to wait, watch, and listen.

Chapter 12

Transformational EMDR Approach to Phases Six and Seven, Body Scan and Closure

EMD for the Body, Somatic Bridge, or Go with That

Carolyn Lenz, LMHC

Physical sensations and somatization often emerge during the closing of the session, particularly when we complete a body scan in Phase Six. Regardless of whether Phase Five was fully completed or not, we always close the session by completing the body scan. The therapist will invite the client to think of the target and scan their body (head to toe) to see if any uncomfortable or unusual sensations are present. If the client identifies any distressing sensation(s), then we will complete EMD focused on the body to reduce or resolve them.

When an uncomfortable or unusual sensation is noted by the client (in Phase Six), the therapist should first briefly explain how they will work with that in Phase Six. The T-EMDR therapist *works with the client, not on the client.* Simply explaining, "the sensation(s) is some lingering activation in your body, and we are going to do a few short passes of the DAS to help resolve that." Usually that is all it takes.

Then the therapist invites the client to "focus on the

sensation and notice if it changes." While the client does this, the therapist administers short sets of DAS, then stops the stimulation and asks the client, "Has anything changed with the sensation(s)?" Do not say sensation; identify the body sensation in the query. For example, let's say the client has a headache. The query will sound like this: "Has your headache changed in any way?" If the client says no, continue with the stimulation. If they say it seems to be hurting less, the query is, "Okay, notice that it is hurting less. Go with that." This process is repeated until the sensation is resolved or the client reports it is no longer distressing to them.

It is essential to keep the sets brief and use the query, "Has anything changed with the sensation (repeat the sensation)?" rather than "What are you noticing?" The reason for this is that during Phase Six, we are using EMD to desensitize any lingering activation and close processing, as opposed to EMDR, where we are trying to link the sensation to unresolved associations, which opens channels for processing. Often, with just a few passes of EMD, the sensation is cleared. However, sometimes these sensations can be quite active before the body clears them.

For example, I was working with a sexual assault survivor who, during the body scan, noted the sensations moving to other areas—her throat, her arms, her wrists, her legs, and eventually even slightly outside of her body, then back in. However, after about ten-twelve sets of EMD, the sensation completely left her body, she was no longer in the space around her, and it had fully resolved, which led to great relief for her. Although I couldn't logically understand how she could feel an uncomfortable sensation outside of her body, that is what she reported. I went with it until she reported that it was entirely resolved. The T-EMDR therapist understands that we don't need to understand; we follow the client and trust the self-healing process of T-EMDR to do its job—if we just stay out of the way.

If a client quickly processes through Phase Four and Five and has intense physical sensations in Phase Six, this can be an opportunity to use the somatic bridge/floatback technique. By using the somatic bridge, we are able to float back to an earlier time when the client experienced this sensation, which can open a new or previously unresolved channel of association. If a connection is made, then we go with it (with the client's consent). If the somatic bridge connects to something but the client does not want to proceed with it, make a note to discuss in Phase Eight, during the following session, and continue with standard EMD for the remaining sensations until Phase Six is complete. The bridge must be used only in Phase Six if adequate time is available to process any material that is discovered. Additionally, I find that if sensations emerge during Phase Four and the somatic bridge is successfully utilized, there tends to be less or no activation remaining by the time we reach Phase Six.

As the therapist, you are responsible for time management and ensuring that the client can work through what they need to and close the session feeling stable. This final phase of actively processing sensations is critical and should not be overlooked. I had a client tell me that their former EMDR therapist would just end the session when time was up and ask them to do the body scan or container on their own. A client should never be put in this position!

As a T-EMDR therapist, you understand how the body communicates, how to follow the client, and how to provide support to your client as they work through these deeply vulnerable and powerful experiences. Phase Six is the final step to helping your client resolve any lingering distress that might still be active. By using the T-EMDR processes we have explained, it is likely that, by the time you reach Phase Six, there will be little to no activation remaining in each phase of EMDR.

Phase Seven closure

Closure is phase seven of Shapiro's eight-step model. Most of you should know how to inform your client about what they can expect after an EMDR processing session. We tell them that processing continues and that they may continue to experience things over the next week, which can include memories, images, thoughts, feelings, and body sensations. The T-EMDR therapist asks the client to write anything of note down to discuss in the next session. If they notice something distressing, they should call and come in immediately. One thing that all T-EMDR therapists do is to remind the client that their sleep might be impacted. Some people sleep better, and some have interrupted sleep. It is nothing to worry about, as it is temporary. The client is always informed that they may have more vivid dreams or even nightmares. Again, this is no cause for concern; this is temporary. EMDR is reorganizing your life experiences, and it does some of this work at night.

The T-EMDR therapist knows how vital the subtle warning about nightmares is in closing out the session. This explanation is needed for two reasons: First, if you do not mention nightmares and they have nightmares, they often want to stop doing EMDR. Normalizing the nightmare prevents this problem. Second, if they do have nightmares and you told them, they might have a nightmare, which brings credibility to your skill and your understanding of what can happen during EMDR. Always mention, but do not emphasize and make a big deal out of it. You don't want to scare them away.

Chapter 13

Transformational EMDR Approach to Phases Eight and Nine

Introducing Phase Nine—Target, Emotion, Negative Cognition (T.E.N.)

Robert Engle, LMHC

Why a Phase Nine?

When Francine Shapiro introduced Eye Movement Desensitization and Reprocessing (EMDR) in 1989, it was not presented as a comprehensive theory. In fact, it was not even called EMDR; it was called EMD because Shapiro initially thought she was simply desensitizing a memory or an image—a method to resolve disturbing traumatic memories. Her early texts outlined eight phases: history-taking, preparation, assessment, desensitization, installation, body scan, closure, and reevaluation. The first book, *Eye Movement Desensitization and Reprocessing* (EMDR) *Therapy: Basic Principles, Protocols, and Procedures*, was published in 1995. At this time, EMDR was seen as a procedure for the treatment of trauma that had to be integrated into the models clinicians were already using. In 1995, everyone had their models, and they headed to figure out how to add EMDR.

It was not long before Shapiro realized there was more

happening than desensitizing a memory. By 2001, Shapiro described EMDR as a comprehensive psychotherapy model grounded in the Adaptive Information Processing (AIP) framework. This evolution marked a paradigm shift: Human beings are not only wounded by isolated events but shaped by maladaptive networks of memory, belief, and affect. EMDR was no longer simply a tool for trauma but a way of understanding the psyche, healing, and transformation itself.

If EMDR is only a treatment for a single-episode trauma, as it was initially thought, eight phases are sufficient. But if it is a model—a living framework of how the mind heals—then we must notice that healing rarely stops neatly at Phase Eight. Clients do not simply resolve a target and walk away whole. Life continues, the unconscious keeps speaking, and new material surfaces in the days and weeks between sessions.

Carl Jung foresaw this dynamic decades before EMDR. He wrote:

> Everything in the unconscious seeks outward manifestation, and the personality too desires to evolve out of its unconscious conditions and to experience itself as a whole (Jung, 1953/1968).

> If you bring forth what is within you, what you bring forth will save you. If you do not bring forth what is within you, it will destroy you (Meade, 2016).

The unconscious does not respect the borders of phases or protocols. It communicates whenever it finds an opening—

through dreams, irritations, slips of the tongue, or synchronicities. EMDR provides us with tools to recognize these moments. To honor them, we must realize an implicit phase that bridges the formal protocol with the ongoing conversation of the unconscious.

This missing link is the space that Dr. Andrew Dobo has called the "Lost Phase Nine." It is the mystery between the end of Phase Eight and the beginning of the next Phase Three. In this chapter, I present Phase Nine as both a bridge and an invitation: a way of listening to the unconscious as it continues to guide the healing process.

Phase Eight as checkpoint—Phase Nine as doorway

In standard EMDR, Phase Eight is reevaluation. Shapiro was clear:

> Reevaluation is not merely a formality; it is essential. It confirms the work accomplished, identifies any residuals and guides the next steps of treatment (Shapiro, 2018).

Phase Eight functions as a checkpoint: Are SUDS still low, VOC still strong, body tension resolved? But in Transformational EMDR, Phase Eight is more than a checklist. It is a threshold moment. Within the disease model, Phase Eight can look like an ending: "Are the symptoms gone? Good—we are finished." But in a transformational lens, Phase Eight is a doorway into individuation. It is the pause where we listen for signs of where the client stands in their larger arc—a framework described later in this book as avoidance, surrender, dismantling, chaos, rebirth, and assimilation. These stages are not part of Shapiro's original eight-phase model but come from the Transformational EMDR emphasis on individuation and ongoing growth.

This is where Phase Nine begins. Clients often enter a reevaluation session reporting stability: "I feel lighter," "I slept better," "The memory doesn't bother me." Yet just as often, they mention something seemingly mundane:

> "Someone cut in front of me at the grocery store."
> "My neighbor's dog wouldn't stop barking."
> "I ordered broccoli with cheese, and it bothered me because I cheated on my diet."

To the untrained ear, these sound trivial. However, through a Phase Nine lens, they are the unconscious speaking. As Jung observed: "Until you make the unconscious conscious, it will direct your life and you will call it fate" (Jung, 1959/1969).

Phase Eight ensures stability; Phase Nine opens the door to what fate is presenting in the here and now or where the past is still present for the client.

Ongoing history-taking

Most therapists associate history-taking with Phase One, where a client's past traumas and anchors are mapped. But in Transformational EMDR, history-taking is ongoing. Phase Nine is this living history-taking: listening to what the unconscious presents after previous targets have resolved. Shapiro herself hinted at this unfolding when she wrote:

> Once the information has been fully processed, the system continues to make the appropriate connections on its own. Adaptive resolution becomes the foundation for ongoing growth (Shapiro, 2018).

Processing continues outside the session, and Phase Nine honors this by treating a client's daily experiences—such as dreams, irritations, and synchronicities—as new entry points. A client might say:

> "I thought I'd lose my mind at the sound of that barking dog."
> "In traffic, I couldn't believe how angry I got."

The T-EMDR therapist does not dismiss these irritations. Instead, they hear them as tributaries of unresolved Emotion. As Shapiro reminded us, "When dysfunctionally stored information is triggered, the past becomes present" (Shapiro, 2018).

The essence of TEN: Targets, Emotions, Negative Cognitions

Phase Nine becomes truly practical through the framework of TEN: **Target, Emotion, Negative Cognition.** These three pieces form the backbone of any EMDR protocol, but in Transformational EMDR, they also serve as the lens that helps us identify what the unconscious is offering in Phase Nine.

Francine Shapiro built EMDR around an eight-phase structure that gave therapists a detailed map. Dr. Dobo recognized that when working in the spontaneous, sometimes unpredictable space of Phase Nine, clinicians needed a simpler guide. He distilled the essence of Shapiro's framework into three elements—the minimum ingredients required for reprocessing to occur. In doing so, he gave therapists a reliable way to catch Phase Nine material in the moment rather than dismissing it as trivial.

TEN is both shorthand and a compass. It reminds us that if we can identify a target, recognize the Emotion, and name the Cognition, we have all we need to engage the protocol—whether the entry point is a childhood trauma or an offhand irritation from the grocery store.

- **Target** is the event, image, or symbol that the unconscious brings forward. It may be as small as being cut off in traffic or as fleeting as a dream image.
- **Emotion** is the affective charge attached to that target—the anger, shame, fear, or sadness that signals unfinished business.
- **Negative Cognition (NC)** is the old belief that lies beneath the surface: "I don't matter," "I can't control anything," "I'm not safe," "I'm not good enough."

Together, these three elements unlock the pathway to processing.

Consider two everyday examples:

A grocery store slight becomes:
Target: being cut in line.
Emotion: anger, hurt.
NC: "I don't matter."

A barking dog becomes:
Target: relentless noise.
Emotion: helplessness, frustration.
NC: "I can't handle it."

At first glance, these experiences seem too minor for therapy. But when framed through TEN, they reveal the same structure as trauma targets. What looks trivial is in fact the unconscious presenting—offering a thread that, when pulled, can unravel deeper maladaptive networks. Dr. Dobo often reminds therapists: *"There's the Target, there's the Emotion, and there's the Negative Cognition. That's the essence of a protocol. And it doesn't have to be a trauma."*

Here Jung's wisdom becomes indispensable again. The unconscious rarely speaks in plain language. It speaks symbolically, often cloaked in metaphors, slips of the tongue, or dreams. A client saying "I feel like I'm drowning" may not describe a literal event, but the phrase itself functions as a target. The affect of panic is the Emotion. The cognition might be "I can't handle it." In Phase Nine, these moments are not just metaphors; they are invitations. They open the door to the client's truth.

By listening through the structure of TEN, therapists learn to treat everyday irritations, dreams, and symbolic fragments as legitimate material. TEN strips Phase Nine of mystery without reducing its depth. It keeps the work simple, direct, and actionable—ensuring that whatever the unconscious brings can be recognized, named, and transformed.

Hearing Phase Nine: listening differently

If TEN gives us the map, *listening differently* is how we use it. Phase Nine is not so much something we "do" as something we *hear*. In Dr. Dobo's trainings, he often uses a guiding phrase: "Wait. Watch. Listen." It captures the therapist's stance of letting the client lead with what matters most. This phrase refers to the stance or posture a therapist adopts, allowing the client to lead with what is important. Here in Phase Nine, it is essential to allow the client to share and for us to listen to unconscious material they may not even be aware of.

In standard EMDR practice, Phase Eight can become procedural:

- "Is your SUDS still at zero?"
- "Is your VOC still strong?"

If the answers are positive, the therapist may simply move on to the next planned target. But Transformational EMDR requires a different stance. The therapist listens for the three pieces of TEN hidden in ordinary stories. A client who says, "I was in traffic and someone cut me off" is not just making small talk.

They are presenting:

Target: the cut-off moment.
Emotion: anger, frustration.
Negative Cognition: "I don't matter," or "I have no control."

A conventional ear might dismiss it as a common annoyance and move on to their "plan" of a more significant traumatic event. Dr. Dobo warns of dismissing what walks in the door. This is not only Dr. Dobo saying this. Shapiro says it as well.

> When we first started, we had lots of clinicians who understandably saw the big *T* trauma that you needed to diagnose PTSD, and you can easily see rape, kidnapping, car accident, the big ones having a negative effect. We're trying to sensitize clinicians to, just because it's not these big criterion *A* ones, don't forget about those other experiences, those more ubiquitous ones of being humiliated in grade school, of being pushed away by Dad, of having these losses, of having all of these things that go through childhood. Realize they're going to have those negative effects also, and if they still have negative effects, you think of them as a trauma, because by dictionary definition, they had a negative effect upon self or psyche (Shapiro, 2003).

A transformational ear recognizes it as the next target. Francine Shapiro cautioned against dismissing what emerges in the present:

> Clinicians must follow the client's process without interference. If you allow the client's memory network to unfold, it will go where it needs to go unless it becomes stuck (Shapiro, 2001).

Listening differently means assuming that what the client brings is never random. Phase Nine is about catching those offerings and mapping them through TEN.

Jungian integration and the language of the unconscious

Dr. Dobo discussed the importance of learning to hear unconscious language, especially in Phase Four, but your ear should be tuned to hear this language in all phases of EMDR. Let us look at its value in Phase Nine. How does one listen differently?

Jungian psychology explains: The unconscious speaks in its own language—symbols, metaphors, and images—and TEN gives us the tools to translate it. Dr. Dobo frequently reminds his trainees that the unconscious is speaking to us all the time, even while we sleep, or perhaps especially while we sleep. However, you have to learn its language because the unconscious doesn't text.

Jung emphasized that the unconscious is not a neutral backdrop; it operates both as an adversary and as an ally in the process of individuation. He describes the unconscious as being amoral; in other words, it does not make the news, it simply reports the news. It is incapable of deceit. We usually resist the truth about ourselves. Early in life, or when defenses are strong, the unconscious can feel hostile. It presents as chaos, resistance, or self-sabotage, the very forces that keep clients stuck. Nevertheless, once acknowledged and engaged, the unconscious shifts roles. It becomes a collaborator, continually offering fragments of unresolved material in symbolic form.

He warned: "Until you make the unconscious conscious, it will direct your life and you will call it fate" (Jung, 1959/1969).

Phase Nine embodies this paradox. What the client brings—whether a complaint, a cliché, or a dream fragment—may initially appear to be resistance or triviality. But if recognized through TEN, it is revealed as an offering: the unconscious inviting us to continue the work.

When we say the unconscious becomes an ally, what exactly do we mean?

The unconscious is always speaking to us, trying to assist through the client, during EMDR processing, through unconscious language or synchronic events that often seem to have the outer world conspiring to assist the client on their journey.

This is why learning the symbolic language of the unconscious is so vital.

Everyday speech is full of archetypal material:

- Clichés: *"Hanging on for dear life." "I'm always on thin ice."*
- Metaphors: *"I feel like I'm drowning." "It's like walking on thin ice."*
- Colloquialisms: *"I'm hanging on by a thread." "I was running from pillar to post."*
- Common Phrases: *"I can't see ahead." "I got to get out of here."*
- Symbols and images: barking dogs, broken glass, flooded rooms, black walls, raging rivers.

Clients often dismiss these as "just a saying," but in reality, they are coded communications. When therapists map them through TEN—naming the Target, identifying the Emotion, clarifying the Negative Cognition—these phrases transform from background noise into portals for reprocessing.

As Shapiro observed:

> Symbols become clear, insights occur, lessons are learned, and various stages of emotional resolution are experienced, albeit in an accelerated fashion (Shapiro, 2018).

Phase Nine is where Jung's ally/adversary dynamic and Shapiro's AIP model converge. The unconscious may feel adversarial when its symbols are ignored, but it becomes an ally the moment we recognize them as invitations.

For those who want further practice, see the Appendix

for an extensive (though not exhaustive) list of clichés, metaphors, colloquialisms, symbols, images, and hackneyed phrases that can serve as examples of Phase Nine material.

Shadow, fragments, and doorknob confessions

Not all Phase Nine material arrives in polished form. Sometimes it slips in as fragments or last-minute remarks—the very places where the unconscious sneaks past the ego's censor.

Clients often minimize these moments:

- "It's silly, but I can't stop thinking about that barking dog."
- "Weird dream last night about broken glass—probably nothing."
- "Oh, one more thing ..." as they reach for the door.

Jung called these glimpses the **shadow**—the disowned parts of the self—pressing for attention. He wrote: "Everyone carries a shadow, and the less it is embodied in the individual's conscious life, the blacker and denser it is. Yet the shadow is ninety percent pure gold" (Jung, 1954/1969).

Shapiro described them as **implicit memory fragments**, emotions and sensations without full context. She explained: "These fragments of memory can surface as disturbing thoughts, emotions, or physical sensations without the client being able to link them to an original event" (Shapiro, 2001).

When heard through TEN, even these fragments are sufficient to begin:

- **Target:** the dream, phrase, or minor event.
- **Emotion:** the affect it stirs.
- **Negative Cognition (NC):** the old belief in new disguise.

Doorknob confessions, minimized irritations, and stray dreams are not side notes. They are Phase Nine in its purest form: the unconscious pressing material forward, trusting the therapist to listen. These vignettes remind us that Phase Nine is not about finding the extraordinary but about recognizing the extraordinary hidden in the ordinary.

Case applications of Phase Nine

The following vignettes come from real clinical work, with identifying details altered for confidentiality. These examples are simplified but reflect the actual application of Phase Nine in clinical practice. They illustrate how ordinary events, when heard through the lens of TEN, open directly into unresolved memory networks.

Take the **grocery store incident**, where a client fumed after being cut in line. On the surface, it was an annoyance; mapped through TEN, it revealed the Target (being invisible), the Emotion (anger and humiliation), and the Negative Cognition ("I don't matter"). Processing quickly connected to earlier memories of neglect within her family system.

Or consider the **barking dog**, which a client described as an unbearable noise from a neighbor's yard. The Target was the dog's relentless barking, the Emotion was helpless frustration, the NC "I have no control." Once processed, the barking led straight into childhood experiences of living in a chaotic home where her needs were ignored. The same pattern has appeared in other, equally ordinary circumstances: A client once described feeling "crushed" when their manager failed to reply to an important email. The Target was the silence of the unanswered message, the Emotion shame and anxiety, and the NC "I'm unworthy." What began as workplace frustration unfolded into early memories of being dismissed whenever they sought attention at home.

Another client casually mentioned, "Everyone at work went to lunch without me—it's no big deal." The Target was the exclusion, the Emotion sadness and loneliness, the NC "I don't belong." That small remark opened the door to adolescent experiences of rejection and longstanding beliefs of being an outsider.

Sometimes the unconscious speaks through objects. One client arrived flustered after their washing machine broke. The Target was the breakdown itself; the Emotion was overwhelmed and frustrated; and the NC said, "I can't handle life." Processing revealed parallels with a childhood marked by instability, where nothing felt safe or reliable.

Even traffic can serve as the portal. A parent recounted seething in the school pickup line when another car cut ahead. The Target was the intrusion, the Emotion anger, the NC "I don't matter." Beneath the traffic jam lay a lifetime of invisibility within their family of origin.

And in a quieter moment, a client admitted almost offhandedly, "My best friend forgot my birthday, but it's fine." The Target was the moment they realized they had been forgotten, the Emotion loneliness, the NC "I'm not important." That single oversight carried the weight of countless wounds, each one echoing the same unmet need.

Across these stories, the pattern is unmistakable: the unconscious uses the present to echo the past. What looks small—an unanswered email, a broken appliance, a missed invitation—contains the full structure of TEN. Each one is an invitation, and when honored, each becomes a pathway into deeper healing.

Synchronicity and the world as an unconscious ally

Synchronicity is described as a meaningful coincidence. This often occurs with people in therapy, especially if they attend to their dreams. The dreamer may see something during the day while awake that they dreamt about the previous night.

Recently, during a training session with Dr. Dobo, a trainee—Nichole—was discussing her timeline, deciding what she would process in her very first EMDR session the next day. As we reviewed her timeline, she said, "I might do the first thing I have on my list tomorrow, a car accident I was in." She continued, "I am not going to do this last one."

"Of course, that is fine. Do whatever feels comfortable. What is the last one?"

On the timeline, the last item said, *Joey B.* We asked, "What is Joey B?"

She said, "That is my brother. He died almost two years ago."

We told her, "Of course you don't have to do your brother's death, but let me say, we are here for five days. There are four extremely skilled EMDR therapists here who have experience with such targets, including Dr. Dobo. People often target serious material here, but do what feels comfortable."

That was the end of our discussion. Until she looked around and gasped, saying, "Look!"

Dr. Dobo gives every trainee a name tag to put in front of their seat so everyone gets to know each other. When she turned around, there was a name tent looking right at us, and the name on the tent was Joey B. That was an emotional event for her. She felt like it was a sign from her brother. With that synchronistic moment, she decided to do Joey B the next day. It was grueling, powerful, and healing.

Later, we asked Joey, the young man in the training, if he wanted to be called Joey B or just Joey. He said, "I go by Joey. I have no idea why I put my initial on the tent."

The therapist's role

These vignettes highlight a consistent truth: Phase Nine material is everywhere, but only if the therapist has the ear to recognize it. An unanswered email, a broken appliance, or a forgotten birthday could easily be brushed aside as trivial. What makes them transformative is not the event itself but the therapist's response to it.

The role of the Transformational EMDR therapist in Phase Nine is deceptively simple: to listen, to trust, and to follow. Yet in practice, this requires profound discipline and humility.

Presence and attunement

The first responsibility is presence. A therapist who is preoccupied with plans, notes, or symptom checklists will miss the unconscious whispering through the client's story. Attunement means leaning into the Emotion behind the words, even when the content seems minor.

Francine Shapiro reminded us: "Clinicians must learn to trust the client's system" (Shapiro, 2018). Phase Nine extends this trust. The therapist listens for subtle shifts in tone, symbolic language, or doorknob confessions—knowing these are not tangents but potential targets.

The practice of silence

Another task is restraint. Phase Nine does not ask the therapist to interpret, analyze, or explain. It asks them to hold space, allowing the unconscious to reveal itself. If you just listen, the client will tell you what to do next. You will hear targets all over the place.

Silence here is not passivity—it is active listening, trusting that TEN will surface if we give the unconscious room.

Letting go of the plan

Target-sequence plans and timelines remain useful—especially early in treatment. But Phase Nine invites therapists to set those plans aside when something alive emerges in the moment. A forgotten birthday text, a sudden dream, or a traffic jam may not fit the plan, but they fit the psyche's agenda.

As Dr. Gabor Maté reminds us, "The attempt to escape from pain is what creates more pain" (Maté, 2008). When therapists steer away from what the client spontaneously brings—even if it seems minor—they risk reinforcing the very avoidance that sustains suffering. Phase Nine instead asks us to turn toward these fragments, trusting that they are the psyche's invitation to heal.

The therapist does not—and cannot—predict what the unconscious will bring. By releasing the need to control, they make space for growth that cannot be scheduled.

Trusting the self-healing process

At the heart of this stance is Shapiro's conviction that EMDR activates a natural healing intelligence. The therapist's role is to support that process rather than control it. This process does not stop when the session ends. Many clients describe EMDR as giving them an experience in the therapy room that reshapes how they feel and behave outside of it. A disturbing memory processed in session may dissolve into calm confidence at work, or a long-held fear may suddenly feel irrelevant in daily life. The therapist does not impose these changes; they arise from the client's own system, integrating what was once fragmented.

Dr. Dobo expands this vision: Self-healing is not confined to Phases Four-Six. It unfolds at night in dreams, in traffic jams, or in the grocery store. Phase Nine is where therapists learn to notice and harness that ongoing process, treating the unconscious as a partner that continues the work between sessions.

From expert to facilitator of flow

In this sense, the Transformational EMDR therapist is less an expert who directs the session and more a facilitator of flow. Their commitments can be summarized simply:

- **Be present.** Listen for the unconscious offerings hidden in daily life.
- **Embrace not knowing.** Resist the urge to force a direction or impose a plan.
- **Trust the process.** If the client is speaking it, it matters.

Jung put it succinctly: "The shoe that fits one person pinches another; there is no recipe for living that suits all cases" (Jung, 1957/1969).

There is no fixed recipe for Phase Nine. The task is to create conditions where the unconscious feels free to speak—and then to follow where it leads. In the end, the Transformational EMDR therapist's role is less about directing and more about allowing: being present, listening deeply, and trusting what emerges. This stance not only honors the client's system, it also prepares us to face the larger mystery of Phase Nine—the way healing continues to unfold beyond our plans, our protocols, and even our sessions.

Conclusion: The mystery and opportunity of Phase Nine

Phase Nine is not listed in Shapiro's writings, yet every experienced EMDR therapist is aware that it exists. It shows up in the grocery store irritation, the barking dog, the broken appliance, the forgotten birthday—ordinary events that reveal the unconscious pointing the way forward. Shapiro reminded us that EMDR is not simply a technique but a self-healing process:

> EMDR therapy activates the client's own information processing system. Once activated, the system continues to integrate, creating connections that lead to adaptive resolution (Shapiro, 2018).

Carl Jung, decades earlier, named the paradox: The unconscious can act as adversary when ignored or as ally when welcomed. He wrote: "The unconscious is not just evil by nature, it is also the source of the highest good: not only dark but also light" (Jung, 1959/1967).

Phase Nine lives in this paradox. It is mysterious because it cannot be planned. It emerges unannounced in fragments, slips, or doorknob confessions. And it is an opportunity because when we listen, those fragments become doorways into deeper transformation.

From checkpoints to journeys

Phase Eight functions as the checkpoint: ensuring stability, closure, and integration of prior targets. Phase Nine is the journey onward: opening space for growth, expansion, and individuation. Together, they honor Shapiro's vision of EMDR as a living model of healing, not just a method of symptom reduction.

An invitation to listen differently

For the Transformational EMDR therapist, Phase Nine is not an "extra" phase but a responsibility. It asks us to:

- **Listen differently**: Hear symbols, metaphors, and irritations as messages from the unconscious.
- **Trust radically**: Believe that if the client brings it, it matters.
- **Follow faithfully**: Set aside plans and let the unconscious lead.

As Shapiro insisted, EMDR awakens the client's own healing intelligence. And Jung took this vision even further, pointing toward individuation itself: "The privilege of a lifetime is to become who you truly are" (Jung, 1966/1969).

Phase Nine is where that privilege takes form. It is where symptom relief matures into transformation, where clients move from dismantling and chaos toward rebirth, assimilation, and individuation.

Chapter 14

The Six Stages of Transformation

Explanation and Management of the Six-Stage Transformational Process Out in the World

Dr. Andrew J. Dobo

Now that you have seen the power that is unleashed during T-EMDR, we can understand the language of the unconscious and utilize it. We must discuss the impact of this significant change on the client and their friends, family, and colleagues. I usually warn the client that if we do this work, four things will happen.

1. Your view of the world will change.
2. Your view of others will change.
3. The way you engage the world will change.
4. The way you allow the world to engage you will change.

These changes are what cause the client to begin to move through the six stages of transformation. Each stage has its peril that must be navigated with the help of the therapist and EMDR. Let's review the six stages of transformation.

Six stages of transformation

1. Avoidance
2. Surrender
3. Dismantling the old way of thinking
4. Loss of identity—chaos and confusion
5. Rebirth—begins to accept the new way
6. Assimilation of the new way (Dobo, 2015)

In this chapter, we will move through the stages with an *I don't matter* client. We will describe the problem before EMDR is started—the issues that brought the client into our office. We will then follow the typical *I don't matter* client through the stages of transformation. We will also reference Prince Harry's journey from *I don't matter* to *I do matter* because he is a visible example of what your clients will go through, just in a less visible way, but it is the same. Harry is more visible.

Avoidance is stage one and usually ends when the client walks into a therapist's office. They are in such distress that they will try anything to feel better. The therapist is the "what have I got to lose" person the client comes to see after avoiding their problems in the myriad ways people deny their reality have been tried.

Just because the client is in our office does not mean they are on board. Avoidance is a common phenomenon that therapists have to break through, even when the client wants help. One could write a book about this problem, but for our purposes, we will assume that the client's avoidance has ended when they walk into our office. They are on board and want to engage in the T-EMDR process.

The second stage is surrender. This is essential for T-EMDR to work effectively. As we know, EMDR patients must surrender to the EMDR process. The instruction to the client is that they are not to try to make anything happen, nor are they to prevent anything from happening. They must let whatever wants to happen to happen. In other words, they must surrender to this process. Surrender and let whatever wants to happen to happen.

This is not easy. No one wants to accept that they do not matter to their friends and family. The only time you matter to them is when they can get something from you or you can do something for them. Other than that, you are disposable. No one wants to think they allowed people to treat them like they don't matter and they permitted this treatment to go on for decades. This is the task: to accept your reality, nothing more, nothing less. T-EMDR therapists always tell their clients, "You will not get what you want. You will get what is true." You might want to know that you matter to your father. EMDR will show you that you do not matter to him and probably never will. Alcohol matters to him, not you. Your father's opinion of you has no bearing on your value. The T-EMDR work is to have the client matter to themselves and not to anyone else as a place to start.

How does a person start a life from an *I don't matter* perspective? Well, if we return to Prince Harry, the day he was born, he did not matter. Even though he was dearly loved, especially by his mother, he was the spare. His brother mattered. He spent most of his life being told where to go, what to do, and where to stand. No one cared what he wanted. This is a pretty typical story. Your client with ambitious parents may put work before the child. Work matters, but the child does not. Perhaps the parents are alcoholics or drug addicts; in this case, drugs and alcohol matter, and your client does not. The list goes on and on.

The insidious nature of this *I don't matter* cognition is that, as a child, behaving like you don't matter, being invisible, asking for nothing, and being passive is adaptive if you live with a raging alcoholic who can become violent when intoxicated. So the behaviors that kept you safe and got you out of the chaos alive were effective. As an adult, these behaviors do not work. You are taken advantage of, passed over for promotions, and asked to do things that are not your responsibility, but you go along to get along, as you must have always done. This is how it all begins. It all starts at an early age.

The next stage is the *dismantling of the old way* of thinking. This is when EMDR starts, and the targets are focused around the NC *I don't matter*. As this NC is dismantled, the client changes their behavior out in the world. They see things more clearly. They set boundaries with family and friends. This is when EMDR is often present and future-focused. If the client has to tell a friend who always borrows money and does not pay it back "no" for the first time, that might be not easy. The T-EMDR therapist knows to set up an EMDR protocol on this future event of saying no to their friend. This EMDR session strengthens the client to help them follow through with the setting of this boundary.

Once they begin to build some ego strength, the fourth stage of loss of identity—chaos and confusion—sets in. This happens because if the client says no to the friend, they feel bad; and if they say yes to the friend and give him money, they feel bad too. No matter what they do, they feel bad. EMDR usually has to be administered to address the guilt for simply setting a healthy boundary.

Once this stage is worked through, *the rebirth* or *acceptance of the positive cognition stage* occurs. Once this happens, behaviors that reflect this healthy way of thinking occur more frequently. This leads to the sixth stage of *assimilation*, accepting the new way. At this point, the client is on their true path, making decisions from an *I matter* position.

These six stages are explained in great detail in my previous two books, especially *The Hero's Journey: Integrating Jungian Psychology and EMDR Therapy*. This should give you an idea of what you can expect when using EMDR from this transformational, non-disease-model approach.

Chapter 15

The Plague of Adding to EMDR, Thus Reducing Its Power

Transformational EMDR Therapists Follow; They Do Not Add

Linda Khmelnytska, LMHC

As therapists, most of us are overthinkers by nature. We want to do more, add more, and fix more, especially when we feel helpless in front of a struggling client. We desperately want to help. Sitting in the discomfort of silence or facing the raw edge of a client's pain and doing nothing seems counterintuitive. When we do not fully trust the process, or worse, when EMDR feels "too simple" to possibly be effective, the urge to layer on extras becomes almost irresistible—a little guided imagery here, some affirmations there, maybe a protective figure to insert later. Suddenly, EMDR becomes a Frankenstein's monster of add-ons. However, as the therapist, you feel better. You feel like you did something other than sitting in silence, watching.

The temptation to add to the standard protocol often comes from the therapist's own insecurity. Let's be honest, sometimes we are the ones who feel scared—scared of what might come up. Fearful that we won't know how to handle the unknown, especially when the unconscious and the client's nervous system are about to unearth material in the way it is currently stored. This material can be explosive, bordering on the bizarre. As EMDR therapists, we must expect the unexpected and be comfortable with this unknown material when it arises.

Because we don't fully understand it, we try to prepare ourselves for every possible scenario (just like any overthinker would). We stockpile tools, tack on trainings, and clutter the EMDR model with more and more "insurance policies" against our own fear.

I once met a therapist who told me, point-blank, she was ready to drop $10,000 on another modality because "EMDR just doesn't cut it." That's not about EMDR's limits; it's about hers. The truth is, EMDR doesn't need propping up. But it demands something harder from us: the courage to trust it. To trust us and know that what we need in any given session will present itself, as long as we are in flow.

As Francine Shapiro herself warned, "preparation is not processing"(Shapiro, 2003). When we mistake soothing for healing or confuse comfort with change, we are no longer practicing EMDR—we are just distracting from the work. Every time we tack on extra techniques, we dilute EMDR's transformational power. What looks like "helping" is interference. What feels like more is, in fact, less.

What am I talking about exactly? A trainee who came to one of our trainings reported that she sought out an EMDR therapist to do EMDR. After six weeks, she indicated that they had not yet done EMDR. She explained that her therapist insisted she meet all her parts, which she did not want to do. She did not find it helpful. According to you here at this training, she said, I am supposed to follow the client, which means if I say I don't want to explore my parts—I want to do EMDR—she should abide by my request. That is not what is happening.

This is not an isolated event. I hear these stories when a client comes in for treatment and they say they don't want to do EMDR because they did it with a previous therapist. I ask them to describe what their EMDR sessions were like. What they described bore no resemblance to EMDR. The endless adding in the preparation phases is entirely out of control in our present-day EMDR ecosystem.

Francine Shapiro stopped seeing EMDR as simply another tool to knock down PTSD symptoms or calm a phobia in 2001. In 2001, she knew EMDR was a comprehensive model of psychotherapy as we have discussed. Even beyond EMDR as a model, she presented her aspiration for far more transformational use: EMDR as a pathway to self-actualization. She wanted clients living fully or, in her words, "dancing."

And I've seen exactly what she meant. I've watched clients not just shed symptoms but light up in ways they never imagined possible, laughing again, reconnecting in their marriages, taking risks they once avoided, creating new futures for themselves. That's not symptom relief. That's transformation. And this is where many clinicians often fall short. They treat EMDR like symptom management: another way to soothe, stabilize, or "resource" a client until the next flare-up. But that's not transformation. That's maintenance.

A trainee once came to me asking how to "install a

protective figure" from IFS. Naturally, I was curious and asked about the circumstances. She said she was going to use it in her session that day. I asked, "How do you know you'll need it?" She replied, "Well, it's inner child work, so the client probably needs protection." Probably. That's not client-driven; that's the therapist overthinking, overpreparing, and adding unnecessary stuff to buffer her own anxiety. This way of thinking is diametrically opposed to Shapiro's instruction. "Allowing processing to progress unimpeded can be extremely difficult for many clinicians" (Shapiro, 2018).

The therapist must also surrender to the process by allowing it to play out unimpeded.

Shapiro tells us that, "Clinicians must resist any preconceived notion or interference in relationship to their thoughts and ideas." Their job is to allow the client to "self-heal" (Shapiro, 2018).

After the session, she admitted her client didn't need protection at all. The client figured it out on their own—no protective figure required. No therapist micromanaging. Just the client's system doing what it's designed to do—self-heal. When we predetermine what we are going to add to the standard EMDR protocol in advance, "just in case," we're not listening to what the client actually needs in the moment. By preparing this one thing you think they will need, you cut yourself off from everything else. Everything you ever read, heard, or thought can be accessed if you are in flow. Once you have a rigid plan of what is going to happen in a session, adding this one thing, you lose everything else.

T-EMDR unleashes the client's ability to rewire itself, not just to reduce suffering, but to open space for joy, connection, and authentic meaning. It is not about helping someone manage life from the sidelines. It is about creating the environment for them to step back into the world anew. When you trust the process, you are not just helping someone desensitize a memory; you are watching them reclaim a self they did not even know was possible. Now whole, unburdened, and free.

Every time we add to EMDR, we are not strengthening it; we are interrupting it. Francine Shapiro warned us about this years ago. When we layer on hypnosis, guided visualizations, ego-state scripts, or endless resourcing, we hijack the very thing EMDR is built to do, and that is process the material the way it is currently stored.

She even gave us the metaphor: Resources can be a Band-Aid. They might soothe the moment, cover the wound, or calm the affect, but they do not actually clear the dysfunctional networks underneath. The system is still firing off the same channels. The Band-Aid calms things for an hour, but the channel is not cleared. It simply lies dormant, waiting to be activated until the entire channel is allowed to process the material in the current storage format.

Clients can feel the difference. They leave those sessions saying, "I felt good in the room," but then admit nothing shifts outside of it. Shapiro said her institute was flooded with calls from confused clients, who claimed the "EMDR" they were receiving did not match what they had read in her book. Her complaint was made in 2003, and the problem has worsened significantly since then.

I've seen it in my own practice. A client once came to me after months of EMDR with another clinician. She described sessions that included affirmations, guided imagery, and breathing exercises as part of the standard protocol. She said, "It was wonderful in the moment, like a brain massage, but by the next week, I was right back where I started." That is not processing. That is Band-Aid therapy dressed up as EMDR. Once we stripped away the extras and trusted the protocol, her system did what it was built to do—self-heal. Furthermore, for the first time, her life began to change between sessions, not just during them. She later added, "You did not talk much at all, Linda." I replied, "No, nothing I can say will heal you. The less I say, the more you heal."

That is the danger of adding. It feels therapeutic. It makes the therapist feel useful and the client feel better temporarily, but it does not heal anything. It tells the nervous system, "You cannot handle this without me," when the truth is the system is more than capable if we would just stay out of the way, as Shapiro instructed over and over again.

Every "extra" technique you tack on is really subtracting. It subtracts from the integrity of EMDR, from the client's trust in their own healing system, and from the possibility of lasting change.

Francine Shapiro did not just hand us a protocol; she handed us a mirror. Her challenge was brutal but straightforward: Can you tolerate your client's distress, or are you giving them the same old message they have heard their entire lives?

Shapiro asked, "Are you telling your client, "Don't feel; be afraid of your feelings"? Are you giving them the same messages that they got early on: "Don't feel it. Don't express it..." Because processing means the client will go where they need to go, and are you ready to let them do that? (Shapiro, 2003).

This is where so many therapists stumble. We see the tears start, the body shake, the breath hitch, and our fear kicks in. We scramble for tools, resources, or soothing interventions, not because the client cannot handle it but because we cannot. In that moment, our fear whispers: "If I do not fix this, they will fall apart." However, Shapiro was clear: It is not our job to fix. It's our job to trust the process.

True transformation requires courage not just from the client, but from the therapist. Courage to sit in the unknown. Courage to witness pain without running from it. Courage to let the Adaptive Information Processing system do the work, even when it looks messy, slow, or unbearable.

During Phase Four, one of my clients was shaking and shivering, started gagging, and it was going on for a while. It felt like torture for both of us. There were moments when I questioned whether I had to rescue her and what resources I should employ, but I didn't. She was working through childhood sexual abuse. When we trust the process, the most beautiful things happen. When I was thinking there was no way, she was imagining that her abuser's sperm turned into piranhas and ate him, and left his head to explode. I had no clue what was happening, but all of a sudden, her entire body seemed to melt; she spread her shoulders and became calm. I could have interfered with so many resources right there because I had gotten scared. I chose to trust the process. She was reborn after that session. She was exhilarated and free.

And let us be honest, this is not "doing less." It is more complicated than doing more. Anyone can throw in a relaxation script when they panic. Anyone can toss affirmations at a client to make themselves feel useful. However, it takes radical trust and courage to sit still, track the process, and resist the urge to interfere. That is not passivity. That is mastery.

When we stop tampering, the system surprises us every time. The very moment we fear will "break" the client is often the doorway into their most profound healing. The therapist's courage is what keeps that door open. We must model regulation as they dysregulate.

Transformational EMDR rests on this radical trust. Not trust in ourselves as rescuers, not trust in our bag of tricks, but trust in the system Shapiro built and the wisdom wired into every client who walks into the room.

Francine Shapiro was unrelenting on this point: Fidelity to the protocol matters. Not out of rigidity but out of respect for the model, for the research, and most of all, for the client's own system. EMDR was never meant to be endlessly customized, spliced, or "improved." It was meant to be trusted.

The paradox is simple: Every addition is a subtraction. Every so-called improvement is really dilution. The more we pile on, the less EMDR remains. Moreover, the less EMDR remains, the less transformation is possible.

This isn't about being dogmatic. It is about honoring the integrity of a system that works when we refrain from tampering with it. Fidelity is not a restriction; it's freedom. Freedom for the therapist to stop over-functioning. Freedom for the client to stop being managed. Freedom for the system to function as it was designed to. It was designed to self-heal.

Transformational EMDR is subtraction, not addition. Every time we add, we declare the client's system insufficient. Every time we trust, we unleash what Shapiro built: a therapy that does not just reduce symptoms but sets people free. So, to reiterate, the directive in this book is quite simply to stop thinking, stop adding, and just wait, watch, and listen.

Chapter 16

Transformational EMDR: Utilizing the Dream

Dreams Another Door to Inner Transformation

Ryan Terry, LMHC

I couldn't sleep after my first EMDR session. I tossed and turned in the hotel bed, my head bouncing back and forth on the pillow—much like the blue ball I had followed across the light bar just a few hours earlier. *Processing really does continue,* I thought, reaching for another pillow. Despite the inner agitation, I was smiling as my eyes finally closed. There was a quiet excitement about what I had just experienced, as well as what all of us in the training had experienced. And it was only day two of a five-day EMDR training in Tampa, Florida. The training I had been reluctant to attend was now shifting many of the things I thought I knew about therapy.

I called my wife the day before to try to explain what I was learning and even more what I was unlearning. All I could really manage to say was, "We're not just talking about healing, we're learning to do it!" I felt both giddy and exhausted. Finally, I drifted into a deep sleep.

Then came the dream.

I was back in the jail cell. *The* jail cell. The same place I had used as my target image earlier that day. But it looked different now: brighter, more spacious. I was alone. The feelings of sadness and anger that had long accompanied this image were gone now. In their place was a palpable stillness. I looked around the cell, as if for the first time. Then, I heard something—faint music, maybe? Or the sound of rolling waves?

The cell door was now open.

I walked through it and found myself on a familiar beach. My son, three years old at the time, looked up at me, smiling. He had two paintbrushes in his hands. "Daddy," he said, "I've been waiting for you. Now we can paint the jail the *right* colors!" I followed him back through the open iron doors without a word. On the floor of the cell there were now freshly opened paint cans. Instinctually, I knew what to do, which colors to pick, and which places to work. Blue and orange pastels now covered the cold, hard gray and black. We laughed and laughed until the work was complete.

I awoke gently, tears streaming down my face and onto the sheets. And I was still smiling.

The warmth I felt in that dream has stayed with me ever since that restless night. It was as if that dream was a bow on the session and the full reprocessing that some deep part of me knew I needed. I was changed.

Over the years, my clients have shared similar stories with me about dreams and the semantic meaning they discover as we progress through the stages of Transformational EMDR. As EMDR therapists, we recognize that dreams are often part of the healing process. But as T-EMDR therapists, we engage with them more directly, both during and in between sessions.

Much has already been written about the relationship between dreams and EMDR. Shapiro herself noted the dreams of participants in her very first study in 1989. More recently, Dr. Dobo's books *Unburdening Souls at the Speed of Thought* and *The Hero's Journey* have become essential works, offering practical tools and insights every EMDR practitioner should know.

In this chapter, my aim is not to repeat what has already been so well covered, but to add some color stories, examples, and reflections on the strategies laid out in those earlier works. While we will briefly review some of the core concepts of working with dreams from a transformational perspective, I encourage readers to return to *The Hero's Journey*, especially chapter fifteen, on dream amplification, where Dr. Dobo explores these themes in far greater depth.

My own formal dream work came after a period of crisis I went through in my early twenties. In fact, it was my dreams that led me to seek therapy and then later to become a therapist. It is safe to say I owe a lot to my dreams. I did not have EMDR then, but I was encouraged to respect my dreams. I looked to the works of Joseph Campbell, C.G. Jung, and Marie Louise Von Franz, to name a few. Later, I found Native American elders, Tibetan monks, and a Jesuit priest who also shared techniques that I still use to this day.

In this chapter of the Transformational EMDR manual, Dr. Dobo asked me to share a few examples of my own dreams and the prism through which we try to see dreams as our clients embark on their own hero's journey.

Start with the question

One of the most common things I'm asked by both therapists and clients is, "Where do I start?" The answer is always the same: with a question. After a dream is shared, I begin by asking the client, "What do you make of it?"

At first glance, this may seem too simple. Yet it is essential. If we rush to pull dream dictionaries off the shelf or leap straight into symbolic archetypal analysis, we risk drowning out the most critical voice in the room: the dreamer's own intuitive voice. Even Carl Jung, who was said to have analyzed more than 80,000 dreams in his lifetime, began with the same question. He reminded us that no one knows exactly what a dream means. That is not the nature of dreams. After all, a symbol can hold many meanings at once, and those meanings can shift as we move through different seasons of life. To claim we fully understand a dream would be like claiming we fully understand a tree. Yes, we may know about photosynthesis, oxygen exchange, or root systems, but that does not capture the essence of a tree itself. Dreams work in the same mysterious way–one of a few truths I hope to leave you with after you have finished this chapter. Remember, dreams do not lie. They are incapable of deceit. They only show us the truth.

I am often reminded of what Jung said about true things. "All true things change, and only that which changes remains true" (Jung, 1970). And so, I return to the question: "What do you make of it?"

The dream belongs to the dreamer, and this question is an invitation, an opening into greater awareness. More often than not, clients surprise themselves with the insights that arise when they pause to listen to their own answers. Even when the answer is, "I have no idea what it means," the process has already begun. That admission marks the first step into exploration and collaboration, "the gift of not knowing." Dr. Dobo often mentions and encourages us to be comfortable with not knowing. By not knowing, you become extremely curious and attentive so that this dream or the EMDR process can open a road to knowing. Not so much for the therapist but for our clients. This road is paved with our dreams.

This question, in a sense, starts the party. It creates the space where curiosity, self-discovery, and healing can unfold. Our task is simply to extend that invitation, and then wait, watch, and listen.

Once the dreamer moves to the next stage of analyzing the dream, we can offer our own take and intuitive guidance system. We can share some thoughts, but always with a light touch, following the client's lead.

Taking aim

The late Jungian analyst, Episcopal minister, and prolific author Morton Kelsey recommends three fundamental guidelines for dream work.

Three dream guidelines:

1. Write the dream down.
2. Take the dream seriously.
3. Write it in a dream journal to later work with them.

Dreams have a beginning, middle, and an end. Seeing a dream once it's written or once it has been shared is a nice way to break it down into digestible parts. These are more formally referred to in three parts:

- Part One: The Exposition/Introduction: Beginning, the opening scene.
- Part Two: The Conflict/Problem: This is the meat of the dream, where the action happens.
- Part Three: The Resolution: The *Lysis*, in Jungian terms. The resolution occurs, whether it's a twist or a merging, and it could be joyous, or it's all gone to oblivion; either way, what was there is now resolved in one form or another.

Let's begin with a look at the dream I had after my first EMDR session, with an eye toward these principles and the six stages of transformation that are being mirrored.

I often share Dr. Dobo's reminder that "dreams don't make the news; they report the news." In other words, dreams reflect what we are already wrestling with in our waking life, only in the language of the psyche: symbols and images. They speak in meaning and absurdity, sense and nonsense. The subconscious will use whatever it takes to break through our defenses so that we might remember, reflect, and ultimately change.

In this dream, you can see my own **avoidance** beginning to unravel. I had reluctantly chosen to face what I most resisted, using EMDR and trusting my counselor, my companion, and thus I **surrendered**. The target itself was not even on my original timeline. I had been avoiding it until the very moment I filled out the protocol sheet with my therapist. Still, I knew it had to be faced, and so I surrendered.

The dream carries this movement through the stages. After avoidance and surrender comes the **dismantling**: first, the emptying, the release, no one in the cell, doors flung open. Then comes the **chaos and confusion**: I am lost, unsure, and it is my three-year-old son who must guide me. The roles are reversed. Now he is *my* teacher. At last, he leads me into a **rebirth**, as we paint the cell walls with bright colors, symbols of new life. The cell is remade, and so am I. Something within me has begun to integrate, shifting how I view the past, and with it, how I perceive myself. **Assimilation**, the final stage, is reflected.

Honor the dream in your day

This dream came to me during one of the busiest seasons of my professional life. I was serving as clinical director of a large facility, managing multiple locations and a big staff. At home, my children were still in diapers, and after long commutes, I often had energy only for a short time with them and my wife before collapsing into bed. My self-care had become an afterthought, and my creativity was running on fumes. Looking back, I can see that I was heading toward burnout. That night, as I brushed my teeth, I sighed and told myself once again, "I'll reset next week." Too tired to journal or read, yet again. And then my psyche sent me a lifeline in the form of a dream.

I was in the large living room of a dark house, familiar yet strange. Its corners were blackened by fire, but flickering candlelight revealed marble beneath the charred walls. The rooms bustled with people, split into two tense factions. Though not yet violent, the atmosphere felt fragile. I stepped up onto a table at the center of the room and caught my reflection in a mirror hanging nearby. I was a middle-aged African-American woman. I was elegant and noble, with tired eyes that were older than my body. I cleared my throat, and silence fell. Through tears, my voice rose with strength as I said to the faces looking up at me, "We must come together. A house divided cannot stand."

The mood shifted. The groups began to soften and reconcile.

And then I woke up.

It was one minute before my alarm. I realized I had slept through the entire night, a rare gift in that season of life. Still a little disoriented, I shared the dream with my wife over coffee as we wrangled the kids. Like all the best dreams, it lingered with me throughout the day. I couldn't grasp its meaning, but I knew it mattered.

Later that week I called my sister, Gina. She also takes dreams seriously and is my longest dream confidant. Since we were kids, our mother encouraged us to share our dreams, often at the breakfast table. Thankfully, we come from a family where dreams are sacred.

So I told Gina the dream. "It felt like I was a civil rights leader or something," I said. "Strange, right?"

"No," she replied. "Not strange at all, Ry. Maybe it's an invitation to honor your feminine side." Her words stirred something within me. Curious and inspired, I made a plan for the upcoming three-day weekend. I would make time for both doing and not-doing. Intentionally making time for creativity, music, movement, and reconnecting with close friends I had recently neglected. I informed my supportive coworkers that I wouldn't be checking my email or phone. Each night, I read fiction and journaled. It was delightful.

I returned to work energized, with a renewed sense of purpose. Even as the days grew busy again, I carried those healthy rhythms with me.

Then another dream arrived.

I am back in the house. The same house, once lit only by candlelight, now shines with daylight, streaming through open doors and windows. The feeling is warm and inviting. I walk through the rooms in quiet awe. Despite the burns and restorations, the house feels whole, renewed, and I am proud of it, grateful for its ashes and all. I feel called to the front and look through the wide-open doors. Golden pavers stretch toward a line of trees in the forest. I decide to follow the path, stepping out into the breeze and the sun. The air is sweet, and it feels like springtime. Just as I step into the woods, I see a small nativity scene very much like something you would see outside a church during Christmas. It's empty of figures, but I am drawn to it. I look down toward white linens covering a bed of hay. Drawn to its comfort, I lie down, curling instinctively into the fetal position. I am in a blissful state.

Then she appears. The Virgin Mary, in angelic form. She is radiant and luminous, her skin glowing like a star. She looks down on me with warmth, and I whisper, "Thank you." Her face shifts, first becoming my grandmother's face, then my mother's face, my wife's face, my sister's, my aunt's, and on and on. Each loved female figure who has shined their love on me, in my waking life. I am in rapture now.

And then I wake up.

I still remember writing that dream in my journal the next morning. Even now, recalling it feels like a spiritual experience. It was a big dream. Both were. Dr. Dobo often reminds me of this in our many conversations about dreams. Big dreams can serve as reference points, returning to us with levels of meaning that unfold, even over decades. Sometimes other dreams arrive in support of the original message, echoing and expanding it. But this only happens when we **take our dreams seriously**, when we choose not to turn away in avoidance. The psyche wants to be our ally, not our adversary.

A closer look at the Starlight Madonna dream

This dream is deeply archetypal, rich with universal figures and symbols. The Sacred Virgin appears, radiant with awareness. The house "The Self" stands open, filled with light. Gold, white, springtime, and the manger all carry ancient origins. These things cross time and culture. The presence of

Christmas imagery often signals rebirth, and I have heard such dreams not only from Christians but also from those of other faiths or of no faith at all. In every case, the dream marked a **rebirth** of profound significance.

This one felt as self-evident as any dream I've ever had, but because dreams are sacred, I took my time writing it in my journal that morning. I took my time telling it to a few trusted dream friends and asked Dr. Dobo to make time for a call. "I got a big one today, Doc." I am so grateful to have a tribe of dreamers to do this work with. It is a privilege to allow our clients into this type of tradition that goes as far back as we do.

Later that afternoon, I shared it in full with Dr. Dobo. He still has the recording of our Zoom call. I remember his wide smile, the long pause before he chuckled and asked, "Wow. Well, Ryan, what do you make of that one?" We both laughed knowingly. No analysis was necessary in that moment. When you have a trusted companion to share dreams with like that, some of your analysis won't need any words at all.

Robert A. Johnson, a Jungian analyst and writer, described certain dreams as "confirmation dreams." These are moments when the unconscious, now fully an ally, offers a gift, almost a thank-you from a place at least as deep as your shadow. Dreams like this often appear new in form, yet for the dreamer, they feel undeniably connected to earlier ones, affirming the work already unfolding in the dreamer's life. This is another reason we *write the dream down in a journal.* This will allow for quick recall and reference in light of the new dream, especially one of confirmation.

Again, these are rare, but when they come, they can be

profoundly motivating. If you experience one or hear one shared by a client or friend, celebrate it. However, it is also important to remember that confirmation dreams often signal the beginning of a **rebirth**, and with that comes the call for its own brands of inner and outer work, specifically the type of healing found in Transformational EMDR.

In closing

To share dreams seems fundamentally human to me.

In the end, both dreams and EMDR lead us into the same mystery—the psyche's quiet longing to heal. When we honor the images of night and follow them through the rhythm of EMDR, wounds soften, light returns, and wholeness stirs.

My dreams showed this truth: a divided house calling for unity, a manger cradling me in the radiant presence of the feminine. Each revealed what EMDR so often makes possible—the gathering of what is broken, the uncovering of light beneath ashes.

Dreams remind us, as EMDR does, that the soul is always reaching for wholeness, guiding us so that we can know ourselves deeply and to see ourselves again and again, continually, but for the first time.

Maybe the Lakota elder Billy Mills says it best:

> You have to look deeper, way below the anger, the hurt, the hate, the jealousy, the self-pity, way down deeper where the dreams lie, son. Find your dream. It is the pursuit of the dream that heals you (Mills, 1990).

Chapter 17

Transformational EMDR: A Living Art Form

Where Science Meets Art

Dunja Pacirski, PhD

EMDR therapy is often described in terms of phases, protocols, and neurobiological mechanisms. But for seasoned therapists who practice it daily, EMDR becomes something far more profound than a procedure—it becomes an art form.

When I, like many of us, became a licensed clinician, earning that formal title "practitioner of healing arts," I underestimated the extent to which the therapeutic process would extend beyond clinical skill. I thought I was prepared; I had the protocols, the theory, and the consultation hours under my belt. However, what I did not expect was how healing through Transformational EMDR would require me to become both scientist and artist, technician and soul-listener. I did not know how much of myself I would have to bring: not just knowledge and skills, but patience, intuition, courage, and the creative presence of an artist to sit quietly with the unknown and what cannot be fixed by me. To be a Transformational EMDR therapist is to walk the line between empirical rigor and intuitive artistry.

Beyond protocols: intuitive dance

EMDR starts as a rigid standardized method to be followed in the step-by-step or phase-by-phase format, almost like "painting by the numbers." However, over time and practice, this commitment to fidelity allows the practitioner to flow into their own authentic style of oil painting. T-EMDR therapists receive a thorough and exhaustive training in standardized protocols, techniques, and neurobiology, which allows them to acquire skills at the level of internalized practical knowledge. As Dr. Shapiro emphasized, "the fidelity counts all the time," and she warned that "if you eliminate aspects of the procedure that have been tested, you might be leaving out the relevant brain functions that are necessary to give the most effective and efficient results."

However, once the therapist is comfortable with the EMDR rubric and understands the nature of the EMDR process, the real work begins. Once a comfortable aptitude is reached with EMDR, it leads us to more sophisticated skill development, which starts with sharpening their implicit, tacit faculties, allowing them to create a fluid and adaptive healing space for and in connection with their clients (Pacirski, 2017). As Polanyi (1966) differentiated, in any activity we are focally aware of the object of our activity, as well as having a tacit awareness of that which serves as an instrument. However, he also emphasized that these forms of awareness can be mutually exclusive if one is overemphasized or given too much attention. For example, if a pianist is only concentrating on her key-picking techniques or the mechanics of reading the music in front of her, she will lose the melody. Parallelly, Kondrat (1992), a social work scholar, reflected on a practice situation in which the therapist, who focuses all his attention on the empirically based technique instead of being tuned in to the holistic client's presentation, will describe his performance as staged, and potentially, so will the client.

For instance, my first EMDR trainer, a former pilot by background, provided us with highly structured, blueprint-like instructions, specifying range and exact numbers of sets to differentiate administration among EMD, EMDr, or EMDR. This predetermined number of passes greatly limited my EMDR beginnings, as, before receiving certification consultation with Dr. Dobo, I often found myself counting the sets of bilateral stimulation or insisting on SUDS being zero before starting Phase Five. This has, in return, significantly lowered my capacity to be present in the therapeutic space with my clients and follow their nonverbal cues, "telling" me when to pause or "signaling" an adaptive shift in process.

The practitioner's limited presence and detachment from this subjectively and implicitly based dimension of the shared therapeutic moment can result in overlooking essential cues, disrupting the client's processing effectiveness, and weakening the therapeutic alliance—a recognized key ingredient in any healing process (Kondrat, 1992). The antidote is the mantra you have heard throughout this book. Wait, watch, listen, and follow the client.

Fortunately, my EMDR journey continued with Dr. Dobo's guidance, who insisted on emphasizing my capacity "to be fully present with my clients." Just as a pianist moves within a structure while improvising with soul, T-EMDR therapists navigate the well-mapped landscape of trauma processing with intuition, creativity, and humility. Non-negotiable emotional attunement demands hearing not just clients' words, but their silences, hesitations, and glimmers of insight. It is here, in these subtle spaces, that T-EMDR becomes an art of intuitive healing dance.

The therapist as an artist: mastering the rhythm of silence and being in the unknown

A skilled T-EMDR therapist learns to become a channel, not a fixer—allowing the client's inner guide to lead the healing process like an artist who knows that adding too many notes and overdoing a melody can ruin it, or a painter who knows when the canvas is complete. The T-EMDR therapist knows when to intervene and when to hold the space quietly, simply witnessing.

During my doctoral program and dissertation journey, I set out to explore reflective practice and self-monitoring strategies, such as mindfulness meditation and self-reflective journaling, as pathways to cultivating practitioners' implicit knowledge—that innate capacity to be present, aligned, and in the creative flow of healing with the client. In our professional quest for continuous development, we aim to accumulate explicit knowledge, yet we often neglect the parallel need to nourish our practice wisdom and cultivate our inner environment.

Too often, clinical creativity or intuition is believed to be a fixed trait, something one is born with. My research showed otherwise: These implicit qualities are teachable and can be intentionally cultivated. Through daily engagement in practices such as mindfulness meditation and self-reflective writing, participants in my study reported elevated levels of attentiveness, heightened awareness of the present moment, and a noticeably expanded ability to choose how they receive and respond to the world around them, both personally and professionally.

Presence as a foundation

In my dissertation research, practitioners described presence as "a discipline of coming back"—noticing when one's own thoughts or anxieties drifted and gently recentering on the client's lived experience.

One clinician shared, "I realized that being present is more than listening to the words. It is allowing myself to notice the silence, the tears, even my own heartbeat slowing down as I sat with them." Another participant reflected: "When I am fully present, I hear more than what my client says. I hear the pauses, the hesitations, and I sense what wants to emerge."

For me, presence is evident in intentionally eliminating distractions, such as refraining from checking my phone, actively observing the client's breath during processing, and regulating my own emotional landscape to assume responsibility for our healing space. The tacit dimension of presence cannot be codified in protocols; it must be lived. In T-EMDR, presence becomes the invisible canvas upon which healing unfolds as well as the therapist's most potent instrument.

When a therapist is fully present, the client feels both accompanied and free—supported in their pain, and free to let their own healing intelligence emerge.

Patience and comfort with the unknown

Patience is essential because, as the T-EMDR therapist trusts the self-healing power of EMDR, it requires a surrender to the timing. Patience is not passivity but an active discipline of allowing the process to unfold at its own rhythm. As my research participants described it, it is receptive patience—the patience of a beginner's mind, waiting without forcing. One clinician reflected, "My job is not to push my client toward resolution but to hold the space long enough for their own wisdom to surface." In T-EMDR, patience means not rushing a client toward a desired outcome, as self-healing follows its own schedule, not ours.

The therapist's role is to hold the space patiently—as a form of respect for both the client's inner pace and the mystery of healing itself.

If presence is the ground, and patience the posture, then comfort with the unknown is the atmosphere in which T-EMDR unfolds. Participants in my dissertation highlighted how learning to "trust not knowing" was transformative. One clinician explained, "I used to panic if I didn't have the answer. Now I see that the not knowing is actually where the client shows me the way." Another therapist emphasized the value of silent waiting: "I stopped filling the space, and that's when the most powerful things happened."

The T-EMDR therapist is comforted by not knowing

because it is within that not knowing that the answer will be revealed. This idea of not knowing contradicts everything we are taught in school. We are taught to know. If you do not know, then how will you find the answer? Most will say: Go and research, read, study. The T-EMDR therapist has done all of that and knows the answer is not there. The answer is found in the silent world of not knowing and just waiting, watching, and listening. In T-EMDR, comfort with not knowing allows the therapist to hold space without imposing an agenda. The unknown is not an obstacle but a doorway—where deeper truths surface, often beyond what either therapist or client could have planned.

Flow: individually and relationally

Flow, as explored in my research, is both an individual and a relational state. Experienced at the individual level, practitioners described flow as "losing the sense of time, just being with the client, almost forgetting myself." While in the relational sense, flow emerges when therapist and client enter a tacit synchrony—"It felt like we were dancing. I wasn't leading. I wasn't following. We were just moving together." In T-EMDR, flow means that both therapist and client are engaged in a living, improvisational process—like musicians improvising within a shared structure. This flow allows for surprising insights, spontaneous interweaves, and moments of profound connection.

In conclusion, presence, patience, flow, and comfort with the unknown are not separate traits but interwoven dimensions of Transformational EMDR. Presence creates the ground for patience. Patience opens the space for flow. Flow deepens trust in the unknown. Together, they create a silent space where healing is not imposed by the therapist but revealed through the shared process. Allowing silence to speak is a reminder of what Dr. Dobo said earlier in the book, as he quoted Ursula Le Guin. "Only in silence, the word" (Le Guin, 1972).

The art of subtraction: less doing, more being

Whereas numerous therapeutic models prioritize expanding new insights, techniques, or novel behaviors as a means of facilitating continuous development, the integration of alternative models has not only presented significant challenges and problems but has also become a detrimental erosion within EMDR's very own ecosystem.

T-EMDR works differently. It aims to address the issue of unnecessary additions and, in many ways, is an art of subtraction. In a culture obsessed with doing, adding, fixing, and optimizing, T-EMDR offers a rather radical alternative: healing through unburdening or, as Dr. Dobo coined it in his first book's title, *Unburdening Souls at the Speed of Thought* (2015). A careful, precise removal—not unlike Michelangelo chipping away at marble to reveal the form of David hidden within. T-EMDR does not install wisdom—it clears the debris that obscures it. T-EMDR therapists often speak of it as a process of unlearning, where trauma's frozen messages ("I am unsafe," "I don't matter," "I am not good enough") are gently dismantled. The goal is not to add new beliefs, but to allow truth to reemerge and return to old places with new eyes.

Parallel to this core process happening within the client, T-EMDR requires practitioners to learn everything about the method possible, followed by unlearning—releasing the rigid hold onto protocolized instructions and allowing the intuitive power of flow to lead the way. As Dr. Dobo says, the best therapists have a wealth of understanding of EMDR literature and possess a high level of skill; however, they also have other "units of human achievement," as Pat Metheny calls them.

I have used artists, such as painters and musicians, as metaphors for T-EMDR, but remember that Dr. Dobo is a musician. He often discusses how developing musical skills has made him a more effective EMDR therapist. T-EMDR therapists know that solving EMDR practice problems often requires the use of interweaves that are not mentioned in EMDR books. Often, they must be created in the moment, as you will read about Ryan's Chinese medicine interweave, the Christmas elf interweave, or Serena's New York Italian "I cannot take it anymore" interweave. These creative interweaves come from the content of the therapist's life experience and their authenticity. It is not a logical equation it. This flash of genius cannot happen if the therapist is thinking logically. It happens when thinking stops and the therapist is present in the moment, waiting, watching, and listening. We say "that was a stroke of genius" in America. The Germans call it *einfall*, which suggests the idea fell into one's head. The Greeks call it a "Kairos" moment, and in Sanskrit, it is referred to as a "Ksana." The flash of genius shows up in the perfect moment. You must allow it to happen and trust that it will. If you are counting passes or time intervals or thinking about the intervention you want to use because you took a training last week, it will never happen.

I recall a processing with the client who was in the middle of an abreaction triggered by the guilt, haunted by the belief that she "was a bad person" for not visiting her mom and "being there for her" while she was dying. I remember how the words found their way out of my mouth on their own and without any preceding thought process on my part: "Do you think that a bad person would feel guilty about it?" This statement was followed by having a feeling of something like snapping back to a surface moment, and my adding: "Go with that."

The solution often comes from your inner genius, which knows everything you have ever read, heard, or experienced, and if you are in a state of flow, it is all available to you. That wealth of wisdom includes, yet far exceeds, the EMDR literature. As Dr. Dobo has said hundreds of times, "Learn everything you can, and when you get in front of your client, forget everything you know. And wait, watch, and listen." If you do not remember anything else from this book, remember that. Write it down and know this is your task. To reiterate:

Learn everything you can, and when you get in front of your client, forget everything you know. And wait, watch, and listen.

References

Introduction

Shapiro, F. (2003). The adaptive information processing model and case conceptualization. EMDRIA Conference. Denver, CO, United States.

Le Guin, U. (1972). A wizard of Earthsea. Atheneum Publishers.

Shapiro, F. (2018). Eye movement desensitization and reprocessing (EMDR) therapy: Basic principles, protocols, and procedures (3rd ed). Guilford Press.

Chapter 1

Shapiro, F. (2003). The adaptive information processing model and case conceptualization. EMDRIA Conference. Denver, CO, United States.

Shapiro, F. (1995; 2001; 2018). Eye movement desensitization and reprocessing (EMDR) therapy: Basic principles, protocols, and procedures (1st, 2nd, & 3rd ed). Guilford Press.

Chapter 2

Shapiro, F. (2018). Eye movement desensitization and reprocessing (EMDR) therapy: Basic principles, protocols, and procedures (3rd ed). Guilford Press.

Shapiro, F. (2003). The adaptive information processing model and case conceptualization. EMDRIA Conference. Denver, CO, United States.

Klotz, L. (2021). Subtract the untapped science of less. FlatIron Books.

Chapter 3

Hari, J. (2021). Stolen focus. Random House.

Le Guin, U. (1972). A wizard of Earthsea. Atheneum Publishers.

Csikszentmihalyi, M. (1990). Flow: The psychology of optimal experience. Harper Collins.

Wilson, J. (Host) (2024). How I became a storyteller with Michael Meade (Audio/Video Podcast). Jung and the World Podcast. https://www.youtube.com/watch?v=vZNzZYh3Jx4

Voss, C. (2025). Your gut feeling is more powerful than your thinking (Audio/Video Podcast). The Black Swann Group. https://www.youtube.com/shorts/Y2N2RJiovFQ

Kotler, S. (2021). The art of the impossible: A peak performance primer. Harper Collins.

Shapiro, F. (2018). Eye movement desensitization and reprocessing (EMDR) therapy: Basic principles, protocols, and procedures (3rd ed). Guilford Press.

Chapter 4

Dobo, A. (2018). EMDR 50-hour basic training manual [Unpublished manuscript].

Shapiro, F. (2003). The adaptive information processing model and case conceptualization. EMDRIA Conference. Denver, CO, United States.

Chapter 5

Shapiro, F. (2018). Eye movement desensitization and reprocessing (EMDR) therapy: Basic principles, protocols, and procedures (3rd ed). Guilford Press.

Shapiro, F. (2003). The adaptive information processing model and case conceptualization. EMDRIA Conference. Denver, CO, United States.

Chapter 6

Shapiro, F. (2018). Eye movement desensitization and reprocessing (EMDR) therapy: Basic principles, protocols, and procedures (3rd ed). Guilford Press.

Dobo, A. (2018). EMDR 50-hour basic training manual [Unpublished manuscript].

Chapter 7

Shapiro, F. (2003). The adaptive information processing model and case conceptualization. EMDRIA Conference. Denver, CO, United States.

Dobo, A. (2018). EMDR 50-hour basic training manual [Unpublished manuscript].

Chapter 8

Shapiro, F. (2003). The adaptive information processing model and case conceptualization. EMDRIA Conference. Denver, CO, United States.

Gendlin, E.T. (1981). Focusing (Revised edition). Bantam Books.

Rogers, C.R. (1951). Client-centered therapy: its current practice, implications, and theory. Houghton Mifflin Publishers.

Chapter 9

Shapiro, F. (2003). The adaptive information processing model and case conceptualization. EMDRIA Conference. Denver, CO, United States.

Chapter 10

Shapiro, F. (2003). The adaptive information processing model and case conceptualization. EMDRIA Conference. Denver, CO, United States.

Klotz, L. (2021). Subtract the untapped science of less. FlatIron Books.

Chapter 11

Shapiro, F. (2018). Eye movement desensitization and reprocessing (EMDR) therapy: Basic principles, protocols, and procedures (3rd ed). Guilford Press.

Chapter 12

None

Chapter 13

Dobo, A. (2015). Unburdening souls at the speed of thought: Psychology, Christianity, and the transformational power of EMDR. Soul Psych Publishers.

Jung, C. G. (1953/1968). The archetypes and the collective unconscious (R. F. C. Hull, Trans.). Read, H., Fordham, M., Adler, G., & McGuire, W. (Eds.). The collected works of C. G. Jung (Vol. 9, Part I). Princeton University Press.

Jung, C. G. (1959/1969). Aion: researches into the phenomenology of the self (R. F. C. Hull, Trans.). Read, H., Fordham, M., Adler, G., & McGuire, W. (Eds.). The collected works of C. G. Jung (Vol. 9, Part II). Princeton University Press.

Jung, C. G. (1954/1969). Psychology and religion: West and East (R. F. C. Hull, Trans.). Read, H., Fordham, M., Adler, G., & McGuire, W. (Eds.). The collected works of C. G. Jung (Vol. 11). Princeton University Press.

Jung, C. G. (1966/1969). The practice of psychotherapy (R. F. C. Hull, Trans.). Read, H., Fordham, M., Adler, G., & McGuire, W. (Eds.). The collected works of C. G. Jung (Vol. 16). Princeton University Press.

Jung, C. G. (1957/1969). The development of personality (R. F. C. Hull, Trans.). Read, H., Fordham, M., Adler, G., & McGuire, W. (Eds.). The collected works of C. G. Jung (Vol. 17). Princeton University Press.

Jung, C. G. (1970). The development of personality (R. F. C. Hull, Trans.).

Read, H., Fordham, M., Adler, G., & McGuire, W. (Eds.). The collected works of C. G. Jung (Vol. 11). Princeton University Press.
Maté, G. (2008). In the realm of hungry ghosts: Close encounters with addiction. Knopf Canada.
Shapiro, F. (1995). Eye movement desensitization and reprocessing (EMDR) therapy: Basic principles, protocols, and procedures. Guilford Press.
Shapiro, F. (2001). Eye movement desensitization and reprocessing (EMDR) therapy: basic principles, protocols, and procedures (2nd ed.). Guilford Press.

Chapter 14

Dobo, A. (2015). Unburdening souls at the speed of thought: Psychology, Christianity, and the transformational power of EMDR. Soul Psych Publishers.

Chapter 15

Shapiro, F. (2018). Eye movement desensitization and reprocessing (EMDR) therapy: Basic principles, protocols, and procedures (3rd ed). Guilford Press.
Shapiro, F. (2003). The adaptive information processing model and case conceptualization. EMDRIA Conference. Denver, CO, United States.

Chapter 16

Mills, B. (1990). Wokini: your personal journey to happiness and self-understanding. Feather Publishing.

Chapter 17

Kondrat, M. E. (1992). Reclaiming the practical: Formal and substantive knowledge in social work. Social Service Review, 66(2), 237–255. https://doi.org/10.1086/603883

Pacirski, D. (2017). Cultivating tacit knowledge through reflective practice: Self-monitoring strategies as lived and shared by clinical social work practitioners (Doctoral dissertation, Barry University). ProQuest Dissertations Publishing.

Polanyi, M. (1966). The tacit dimension. Doubleday & Company.

Appendix One

Characteristics of Transformational EMDR Therapists

1. Transformational EMDR therapists create a state of flow during EMDR therapy to access the client's own self-healing power.

Flow is the state of mind discovered by Mihaly Csikszentmihalyi. It is where creativity beyond the frontal lobe is accessed. This state allows the client to access the self-healing power of EMDR. Transformational EMDR therapists know how to create, maintain, and work with clients in the state of FLOW.

Flow is the only human experience in which all six motivational neurotransmitters are simultaneously released. The therapist is attuned to the client; the length of sets is determined by the client's exhalations, tracking every piece of data that is being expressed. Transformational EMDR therapists know every set length is different. They do not count; they do not time sets; they do not read scripts; they wait, watch and listen. This is an extreme form of following the client. It is what Shapiro tells us to do to access the self-healing power of EMDR.

> The integrative AIP model underscores a methodology that stimulates the presumed self-healing mode of an inherent information processing system (Shapiro, 2018).

> Resolution of the disturbance is achieved through the stimulation of the client's inherent self-healing processes (Shapiro, 2018).

They do not take notes while the client is processing. You cannot take notes and be attuned to the client. It is impossible. The therapist should also be in the state of flow, and this is impossible if you are taking notes. Transformational EMDR requires in-depth focus on the client. It is as if what they are experiencing right in front of you is the only thing that matters in the world, and that is exactly how it should be.

You can keep a notepad on the side if something unexpected or essential happens, but do not feverishly write down every client response. Your EMDR skills degrade significantly if you write down notes while administering EMDR. This is a scientific fact.

Johann Hari, in his book *Stolen Focus*, interviewed Earl Miller, neuroscience professor at MIT, who tells us that there is no such thing as multitasking for humans. You might think you are multitasking, but you are not. Humans cannot multitask; only computers can do that. In fact, "multitask" was a term developed in the 1960s to describe what computers do

—not humans. Humans "switch" from one task to another. Scientists tell us that switching degrades your ability to focus. If you cannot focus, you cannot attune to your client.

There are three ways that switching degrades concentration: The first way is what is called **"the switching cost and effect."** Basically, this describes the time it takes to get back to what you were doing when you switched tasks. This back-and-forth is not a seamless process. The brain has to think, "Where was I?" and try to figure that out. This cost is compounded with each interruption.

If you are switching from taking notes and then back to administering EMDR therapy, you cannot see the often-subtle information the client is showing you. You are not attuned, and most likely, the client senses your distraction.

The second way switching degrades focus is called **"the screw-up effect."** When you engage in switching, you make mistakes that you would not make if you were not switching. Switching increases mistakes.

The third and perhaps most important loss during switching is called **the "creativity drain"**: When you are switching from writing notes and then trying to administer EMDR, you cannot engage in deep thought, so creativity is stifled. During EMDR, problems often need to be solved on the fly, often creatively, but you are cut off from everything you know because you are taking notes. You are cut off from your inner genius, your collective unconscious, and your creative self because you are taking notes.

Please, if you want to become a master EMDR therapist, stop writing down the client's responses. You do not need to write anything down; rather, be attuned to the client and just wait, watch, and listen.

2. Transformational EMDR therapists do not expand Phase Two. Keep preparation phase to 15-20 minutes (unless there are other ecological factors to consider).

Any unnecessary delay in starting EMDR processing harms the client. Withholding the life-giving treatment that is EMDR harms. Clinicians often think they are doing no harm by not doing EMDR when it is exactly the opposite: They do harm by withholding treatment.

> Because of EMDR therapy's emphasis of self-healing, any premature attempt by the therapist to intervene (by assuming they need extended resourcing when they are capable of utilizing a safe place, thus delaying Phase Four*) may slow or stop the client's information process (Shapiro, 2018).
>
> *parentheses mine

3. Transformational EMDR therapists follow the client in profound ways.

Transformational EMDR therapists know that whatever the client starts to talk about when they walk in the door is more valuable than their "plan." The transformational therapist's plan is always Plan B. What the client walks in the door discussing is always Plan A, even if it seems insignificant.

Transformational therapists know it is not. Planning things out flies in the face of the psychoanalytic nature of EMDR therapy.

> EMDR therapy is a client-centered approach in which the clinician acts as a facilitator of the client's own self-healing process (Shapiro, 2018).

4. Transformational EMDR therapists always get permission to interrupt before they begin.

Transformational therapists know that keeping the client in the self-healing state of flow is essential. They let the client know they might interrupt them right in the middle of their query response to keep them in flow. They know talking destroys flow, so this simple piece of information ("I might interrupt you") given to the client provides the therapist the freedom to manage and maintain flow.

5. Transformational EMDR therapists get the client in Phase Four as quickly as possible (session two or three) and out of Phase Four into Phase Five as quickly as possible.

Transformational EMDR therapists follow Shapiro's lead by spending minimal time on the preparation phase so they can start reducing the client's suffering, which is done by getting the client into Phase Four as soon as possible, usually in session three.

Typical transformational EMDR sessions model:

- Session One: Biopsychosocial, informed consent, explain EMDR, and timeline homework or target sequence plan, as well as build rapport.
- Session Two: Resourcing, then review timeline.
- Session Three: Phases Three-Seven.
- Session Four: Phase Eight.

6. Transformational EMDR therapists never ask unnecessary questions.

They do not break flow, which unnecessary questions will do.

They never ask, "Where do you feel it in your body?" or "What's keeping it from being a zero or one?" This is one area where we disagree with Shapiro. Flow heals, not gratuitous questions that bring a client to their frontal lobe that disrupt flow.

7. Transformational EMDR therapists never integrate another model unless the client leads the therapist to use it to solve problems.

This integrating of other models with EMDR is upside down these days. When EMDR came on the scene in 1989, everyone had a model. At that time, EMDR was a procedure, a tool for your toolbox, because everyone already had a toolbox. There is a great book that does not get much attention these days called *EMDR as an Integrative Psychotherapy Approach*, edited by Francine Shapiro. This book came out in 2002. Experts in various models discuss how they integrated EMDR into their work and model. They had no choice but to figure out what to do with this eye movement thing and how they could use it in the model they had been using their entire career. EMDR was integrated into their models, not the other way around.

EMDR was not a model until 2001. Before that time, most therapists used EMDR as a procedure that they could use for trauma in those early days. In 2001, Shapiro introduced EMDR as its own freestanding model, the adaptive information processing model. There was no longer a need for integration of other models. There was a deeper understanding of what EMDR could do, and its reach was greatly expanded in this second edition of *Eye Movement Desensitization and Reprocessing (EMDR) Therapy: Basic Principles, Protocols, and Procedures*.

Transformational EMDR therapists have an in-depth understanding of every granular element of what happens during a Transformational EMDR session, which is nothing more than the EMDR session Shapiro describes in the second and third editions of her book.

8. Transformational EMDR therapists understand the language of the psyche.

EMDR is a psychoanalytic model. It is not a desensitization model or an attachment model or anything else. It activates a depth psychology response, but few EMDR therapists are interested in understanding the language of the psyche or even know there is such a thing. This lack of understanding is what causes them to say things like EMDR is not enough. It needs help.

There is no problem with EMDR, but rather, there is a gap in the clinician's understanding of how the psyche speaks during the EMDR session. Logical understanding provides about fifty percent of what goes on in EMDR sessions.

Transformational EMDR therapists possess an in-depth understanding of the unconscious mind's language. They understand that nonsense and sense have the same value.

9. Transformational EMDR therapists understand the two negative core beliefs that drive everyone. They understand the real-world implications of these NCs.

Transformational EMDR therapists use the list of distressing events to determine the client's negative core belief. They identify this belief and know that this cognition will ignite the individuation process, which has six stages. They are highly skilled in handling the two cognitions: *I don't matter* and/or *I'm not good enough*. They understand the profound implications that dismantling these beliefs has on the client's world. They are highly skilled in helping the client navigate the six stages in session and also out in the world.

10. Transformational EMDR therapists understand the six-stage process that is required as these cognitions begin to shift.

Dr. Andrew Dobo discovered these six stages. You can read about them in both of his books: *Unburdening Souls at the Speed of Thought: Psychology, Christianity, and the Transforming Power of EMDR* and his newer book, *The Hero's Journey: Integrating Jungian Psychology and EMDR Therapy*. You can also take his advanced EMDR courses that go into great detail about this work.

11. Transformational EMDR therapists learn everything they can, and when they are in front of the client, they forget everything they know. They just wait, watch, and listen.

Some may think I am against learning IFS or attachment to any other model. I am not. I have attended training in all of these models in my career, and I use them when a problem arises during Phase Four. I am opposed to using these other models first, delaying EMDR therapy, which is what the client needs and often wants. I am a fan of learning everything you can learn, but when you get in front of the client, you forget everything you know, start EMDR and just wait, watch, and listen.

12. Transformational EMDR therapists do their own transformational work.

It is widely known that Jung would say you cannot take your client farther than you have gone on the individuating continuum. Transformational EMDR therapists are not encumbered by their negative core beliefs because they have done their own Transformational EMDR work.

Appendix Two

The Adaptive Information Processing Model and Case Conceptualization

Francine Shapiro's Keynote Address, EMDRIA Conference, Denver, Colorado, 2003

As I said earlier in this book, this speech was like my North Star as I stopped seeing EMDR as a procedure and embraced it as a freestanding, comprehensive model of psychotherapy. I know I've listened to this speech while driving to work every day at least twenty or thirty times, as I have evolved into an EMDR therapist who treated practically every client who walked through my door with EMDR, not just trauma clients.

This speech, the second book from 2001, and my consultations with William Zangwill, PhD, were the secret sauce that allowed me to trust and access EMDR's true power. The speech is provided in its entirety below. I want to thank EMDRIA for allowing it to be to shared here.

Francine Shapiro's speech

And all perception and identification is based on the interaction of the memory networks. This is just conceptually what's going on in there for you. And there is a physical resonance, a cognitive process, and vice versa. Remember the yes-no exercise? Close your eyes for a moment, okay? Just close your eyes.

And notice how your body feels. Just get comfortable if you're not, and wonder why weren't you comfortable. Okay, just notice how your body feels. I'm going to repeat a word, and please repeat the word in your mind in your own language, and notice what happens to your body.

No. No. No.

No. No. No.

No. Now, let it go. Blank it out.

Lifestream. Breath. Safe place.

I'm going to notice how your body feels. I'm going to repeat a different word. Again, repeat it in your mind in your own language.

Yes. Yes. Yes.

Yes. Yes. Yes.

Yes. How does that feel? Different? Two words. There is a physical resonance to cognitive process, okay? So cognitive therapy would say it's what you think that causes what you feel.

But what we recognize in EMDR, it's also vice versa. What you feel from your implicit system is going to bring up the thoughts. When you're tired, you think differently.

When you're sick, you think differently. Do you notice,

you don't make any major decisions when you've been sick or really tired? You're not thinking real well. Things don't look as bright.

They don't look as happy. Whatever the physical ... and what's happening as the client, as we walk through the world, and something happens that is similar to an event that was really disturbing, that's not processed. We don't make the cognitive link, but we perceive it. It links into the memory network, and the emotions and physical sensations arise, and we don't know why, so our brain basically comes up with our thoughts about, gee, we're terrible, or this is hopeless, or that's hopeless, and that's the way it's worked. From the implicit, the unconscious perceptions in, we now have our neocortex try to make sense of it, and we've got a whole rationale for something that was because something came in and linked up in our memory network, and the affect came through our body, and boom, now the thoughts are corresponding to the affect.

In EMDR, we're saying you process those earlier events, so you no longer react in that way. So we're talking about perceptual information linkage in what arises. Am I being clear? Okay.

That's why we're looking for the targets. Connections and channels. Going back to this.

This is major. This is the eight phases, the four steps, all of those things; this is major. This is the guide in terms of the processing, that the target is linked to other memories in a dysfunctional network, that the memories feed the disturbance to the target.

Past is present

Remember, we were talking about going down the channel and noticing, wow, where that came from and what the other links were? Those memories are feeding the disturbance this way, but these memories, and they're being fed down as well. So the memories feed the disturbance to the target, and they're fed by the target. You've got them up and down.

These things make this feel worse. This thing makes this feel worse. That's why you need to clean all of these out, because you don't know what's linked in.

Danger of resourcing

And so it's not enough to just target it and do a resource, and they're happy and you're done. It's a nice Band-Aid. It's good preparation. What do I mean by Band-Aid? It's equivalent when people are going through their processing and they hit a target and they do a resource. You just put a Band-Aid potentially over the channels. You're not even going to get down to the [necessary material], because you've changed the affect state. [You interfered with what they needed to do and where they needed to go.]

Do not use resourcing between sessions unless necessary; tolerate discomfort because processing continues

So all of these things that are here are being masked, which is fine in the office but not so fine when they leave the office, and this hypnotic suggestion or ego state work or relaxation or a triggered resource wears away, because that's not the permanent part. The permanent part is processing out all of this information so it's no longer pushing up. So this is what needs to be cleaned out. [Adding resources at this point prevents it from being cleared out.]

Processing is the breaking of old connections and the linking of new associations to form more adaptive networks. That's what the processing does. It's not purging it or just desensitizing it.

Interweaves

It's making new links, so that learning is taking place. And if, when you are processing, you get stuck, you use what I call the cognitive interweave, which people have misunderstood to believe is always just a cognitive thing. No, it's moving in a certain way or imagining what's the difference between how tall you were and how they were or what would you do now, all sorts of things.

Metaphor for EMDR process and interweaves vs. resourcing

What are you doing? You're mimicking spontaneous processing. That notion of the train track going down the track, every set, the train is moving one step along the way, some negative gets off, some positive gets on, and if I'm stuck, it's not moving. I'm going to move to the next stop, that next adaptive network that would have come in, and I'm going to link it in.

Okay? But mimicking spontaneous processing [with an interweave] is a lot different than just triggering a resource, because I just took them off the train.

They're not processing anymore. I've changed their state. Now, can resources, and are they appropriate to be used at a certain time? Yes, but understand what you're doing.

We'll try to get into that a bit more. All right.

Meet the client where they are

You see, the associative connections are defining our sense of self. Good. But those of you that didn't hear me last year, as you look at it, it looks differently. So think of this spiderweb as those neural networks, as those memory networks that are looking in, which ... impress on your perception of what's there, defining a sense of self, defining a sense of safety.

How big is the danger? Now, sure, you need to be dealing with your client of what skills or resources do you have now or do you need now? Where is that person now? Are they a present danger? If you're going to use an interweave, for instance, in order to deal with it, what would you do now? All of these things are great, but this is the way they're seeing it. This is their world. Once the processing takes place, that's what it looks like without the associative network.

Therapists should stay out of the way

You can see the actual size of that danger. All right? But the danger also is to have you push them to only concentrate on safety when they've also had to really deal with their self-image. Have you decided what they should be processing and what they should be feeling? Or have you let them go unimpeded to where they need to go? This is a very important part. It's sometimes really difficult for clinicians to stay out of the way because we want to help.

And we know what's better. But we don't always know what's better. So, if we'll just let the processing take place in the client's own associative network, honor them enough with a sense that their memory network will go where it needs to go unless it's stuck.

And then we have to help. But if it's not stuck, try staying out of the way. Okay? Distortions are to be avoided.

Remember your A, B, C, D: A, adaptive assimilation. B, brain as the body, part of the body. C, connections and channels.

Avoid distortions—process the information as is currently stored

D, distortions are to be avoided. What does that mean? The pathology is based on the information as it's currently stored in the brain. Okay? The symptoms are coming up.

The reactions are coming up from this information the way it's currently stored. The information is accessed as it's currently stored. When we bring together the image and cognition, and identify the emotion and physical sensations, we're placing the laser beams onto this, allowing us to access it in a controlled manner, as it's currently stored.

But we need to make sure we're tracking it as it's currently stored. When we say, "What do you get now?" it's coming up as it's currently stored. And it's supposed to be processed as it's currently stored.

Shutting down the process inappropriately

Which means if you ask the client, you see we had a lot of trouble in the early days, where clients were getting training in cognitive behavior therapy and breathing skills. And so, as the middle of processing, they would start using their breathing technique, and the processing would stop. Because they just brought in another thing and not letting it stay there.

The way it's currently stored needs to be available so that you're able to go down all of the associated channels that need to be processed. We've had clients, and you have them, and you're stabilizing them on benzodiazepines. We know that after you've processed, you need to go back and retarget, and you may find what was a zero is now at a five because the meds suppress the affect, which meant you're not getting to certain channels.

That's why you have to go and process it again. But the thing to keep in mind is that using guided visualization affirmations or whatever techniques you're using to suppress affect is also doing the same thing. So if you find a need for doing this, you need to go back and do it in an undistorted manner. [In other words, if you stop the process, your client will just have to go right back to this same distressed state next time instead of letting them process in the abreaction they are already in. In essence, you are prolonging their suffering.]

Eventually, you must go back and use this standard protocol; otherwise, you haven't used EMDR. You've merged something together, not allowing those channels to be processed. So if you've manipulated it because every time we use a cognitive interweave, we've manipulated it some, right? We brought in the next bit, but we don't know if we may have taken off target a little bit, right? Anytime we tell them to do something that hasn't come up spontaneously, we've distorted it [the process] a little bit.

Do not dilute or distort the process

Well, that means you have to go back and do it in an undiluted manner. But it's not just at the next set you see, it's not just during that session, because remember what I said about long-term going from working well, this is the working. Now the long term may be at the end of the session, but the full consolidation and integration, mm-mm, next week and before termination major memories you've got to go back and check, because if you've distorted it, whatever you've distorted it with, if you've done guided imagery hypnosis, round table, inner child, those are great things, but you know you've distorted it. It's not the processing if you've done them for whatever reason you felt you needed to because the client was going too far away or whatever it might be. You have to go back and make sure you've cleaned it all out, okay? Because those things are like benzos, are going to pass: hypnosis, hypnotic suggestions, pass. Affirmations, unless they're constantly reinforced, pass. What you're looking for is full and complete processing so it's reevaluated as it's currently stored, and at the end of the session you are. If you've manipulated it, that's the way it's coming up. That's why you have to make sure and go back the next time and the time after that to make sure that it's kept in good shape. The bottom line is preparation is not processing.

See, all these great things that I see being suggested in the field—the ability to make more robust the history taking, the preparation, fabulous, just fabulous ways of making reevaluation fabulous—this is great. The more wisdom we can bring in from all different orientations, the better, because we all want the same thing. We want healthy, happy clients that can bond and love and connect. That's what we want, but seeing them with a smile on their face at the end of the session is not it [EMDR]. [That's not EMDR.]

Stop adding to EMDR

We have had an upsurge in clients calling the institute over the past year saying, "I'm really confused. I've been doing EMDR for weeks or months. I love my clinician, we have a great rapport, and I feel great at the end of every session, but when I go home, my issues are still there. I'm just not getting any better, and I read this book, and it doesn't sound like what they're doing is EMDR."

They say, "Well, did you speak to the therapist?" And I said, yeah, preparation is great. Everybody doesn't need a lot of preparation. You know that's the bottom line because the preparation isn't the processing.

Don't overdo preparation

So part of the clinical work is to identify with that client how much preparation does that client need, because they're going to have to be in a certain stance in order to handle/evaluate experiential contributors. It's experiential contributors to health as well as dysfunction. So yeah, there's genetics, no question, yes, there is. I didn't sleep last night very much, and I'm tired, and that's affecting me absolutely. But we're looking at experiential contributors that are stored in the brain that need to be evaluated, accessed, and processed.

Every single one needs to be processed?

No, because we know we have the generalization effect, right?

But they need to be evaluated, experiential contributors positive and negative. What good things have happened to them? What positive people have been in their life? Because that's going to assist in what do I use to help prepare them, what I might use for a cognitive interweave, what relationship do they have with their children. Will I need to bring that in with "what if you're a child?" during a cognitive interweave, you know, positive ones that let us see what they have and what they're going to need.

Shapiro self-actualization: Transformational EMDR

You have to evaluate the difference between symptom reduction and comprehensive treatment. Someone comes in with a driving phobia. If I just concentrate on the driving phobia and send her back to a life of quiet desperation, I wouldn't personally consider that good work unless that's all she's willing to do, but as a clinician, if I'm taking a history and seeing the larger clinical picture, at least let me make the person aware of the possibilities and the potential to see if there's other things, because a symptom like a phobia or PTSD can simply be masking. It's like taking the quilt off the mattress. You know there can be a lot of lumps and bumps that you need to deal with, so if I take a good clinical history, I'm able to identify what might need to be processed to help get this person to an *actualized state.* You know it's like not just actualization for some. Actualization for everyone, into positive; it's not a disease model. We just don't want them to not be limping along; we want them to be dancing.

Okay, evaluate them individually, great. Evaluating them individually, how they are with me and systemically, which means how are they when they are with their family, social setting, larger setting? And for this, we need the feedback.

So it's not this, when we say, in research, you should be able to process a single event trauma in three sessions. That doesn't mean you should, that's all the therapy you should do. It's giving you a rule of thumb in terms of processing, but what you hopefully are looking for is how do I bring these clients to a level that they never even knew was possible before? And is it okay if they go even further than I am? Is that okay for the clinical tapestry?

We're looking for positive and negative experiences, and we want to use every different orientation in order to bring in those possibilities. If you're looking at, if you're talking to a person from psychodynamic, you're going to be looking at family of origin issues. You're also going to have a sense of defenses, right? Great. What is a defense? It's a habitual way that the client, you learn to respond because of survival during the early days. Where did that come from, earlier memory; what are the earlier memories that need to be processed? All of these are to identify where we have to look for in terms of foundation memories. What present situation transference? What does that mean? Their habitual way of responding to people is what they're doing with me, so I can identify from that a habitual characteristic.

What belief [*I don't matter* or *I'm not good enough*] they have about themselves, that's in there. Link it back to the earlier memory. All of it is feedback for the clinician. Behavior therapy, doing a functional behavioral analysis. The last time you were upset, what happened? There's the trigger. What were you thinking? There's your image. What were you thinking about yourself? There's your negative thought. How did you feel? There's your emotion. Where did you feel it in your body? There's your sensation. What did you do after that? "I went and drank."

They get to see the connection, and you get to see what types of experiences you're going to need to process, the past, and for the present, cognitive therapy gives you beliefs to use: I'm helpless, I'm hopeless, I'm not lovable, I can't succeed. Where did it come from? I think we've all agreed it's not an alien virus visitation. What earlier experiences set it in motion?

Timeline (list of distressing events): a place to start

Use a timeline. Start from zero. What was going on in family interactions? Then write it down. Year of birth—how were they physically? What comes up for them, not that they remember what happened when they were one years old. What were they told? Okay, which goes back to, do you have to do preverbal trauma? Well, conceptually, everything's linked. Here the experience might be in a soma level, but once you learned language, it's linked in, and these experiences have linked into the others.

So I have plenty of places I can go to process things that are going to go down into earlier somatic pieces. I don't have to go looking for them; they're going to be linked.

[This single sentence rejects the idea of talking to parts, creating attachment figures that the therapists think they might need when the therapist has no idea what they need.]

If they are separate, that's how I'll be worried at the end of therapy if I've done all of the processing and there's still stuff left. I know there was neonatal stuff. Maybe I'll go looking for some stuff, but we're talking small amounts of clients, so it's just something I want to sensitize. If you find that someone had to be in an incubator during the first year of life, you do not have to start with "bring up the incubator." Okay, the way they are in the world of feeling a burden, not good enough, they can't succeed, it's going to be part of the family interaction because the family was scared and overprotective. So they're feeling that they were damaged. Well, they were. This is true. They were damaged at the time. This is a true statement, but what does it feel like for them now? That's why it has to be processed, you see.

Okay, family systems do a genogram, which is a nice thing that [Maureen] Kitchur introduced to a lot of folks who got a doctorate and never saw a genogram. So this is how we know from crossing orientations what we can possibly use. Timeline genogram: why, because you're filling in varieties of different experiences during history-taking. Experiential somatic: How did you feel the last time it happened? Notice where you feel it in your body. Think back in childhood; do you have an earlier thing? When's the earlier time you felt this way? This gives you earlier targets.

Past is present

Why can you go in, in the present? Yeah, but this is what you're dealing with. Remember the disturbance goes down; the disturbance goes up. You're counting on it opening up; if it doesn't open up, you're left with the present situation. Sometimes, the present is more difficult to close down. And it's not moving. It's because these earlier experiences are feeding it. That's why we say go to the past first. Now, if someone was raped, do you always go to the past first? No, you've got a rape. You've got a PTSD situation, but it's good to find if there are other sexual assaults, okay?

Don't ignore small *t* or implicit memory fragments (Don't have to start with the earliest or the worst)

Anything that's happened, get a history. See if there is a reason to go in an identified big *T* trauma in the present. That may be all you need to do; however, it also may be earlier stuff that's feeding it, and that's why you would be going there first. Float back, bringing the EMDR procedures to bring up the image, bring up the negative cognition, notice your body, let your mind go forward. Float back is also going backwards. Go forward to your worst: What's the worst thing you can imagine? What happened? And that also gives you information. Pictures: Have them bring in pictures from their family of origin, sit down and talk to you about it. Hear what they say about it. Early videos can bring up a lot of stuff, and journal artwork. In other words, all across the clinical spectrum, bringing the wisdom of all of the orientations to flesh out what particular targets need to be done is fabulous.

It's great, and the more we can learn from each other, the better, but as we're going through it, it's in service of finding the targets that need to be processed, the negative ones and the positive ones, processing the negative to transform them and incorporating the positive, because if a client was traumatized during her earlier years, she passed through various developmental stages without taking on what she needed to, to have the psychic infrastructure to love, to bond, to connect, to have joy.

We want to be able to bring those in, so processing is processing the negative and positive experiential contributors, the experiential contributors to dysfunction and the experiential contributors to health, so when I hear people say I don't use the EMDR trauma protocol, it's based on a misunderstanding. When we first started, we had lots of clinicians who understandably saw the big *T* trauma that you needed to diagnose PTSD, and you can easily see rape, kidnapping, car accident, the big ones having a negative effect. We're trying to sensitize clinicians to, just because it's not these big criterion *A* ones, don't forget about those other experiences, those more ubiquitous ones of being humiliated in grade school, of being pushed away by Dad, of having these losses, of having all of these things that go through childhood. Realize they're going to have those negative effects also, and if they still have negative effects, you think of them as a trauma, because by dictionary definition, they had a negative effect upon self or psyche. Think of it as a small *t* trauma, but that doesn't make this the trauma protocol.

It's the protocol for processing experiential contributors of dysfunction in health, got it? Okay, A. B, brain, is the body; C, connections and channels; D, distortions to be avoided; E, evaluate every experiential contributor, because pathology is based upon stored experiences, and health is based on stored experiences. So it's not enough to just have processed out the negative; it's where does it need to go now? As I said, the relevant systems in the brain. It used to be really easy. It was the conscious and the unconscious, okay, and that's all we had to worry about. But now we're dealing with the biological, the neurobiological concomitants of understanding that the sympathetic and parasympathetic system, those involved in fight or flight, how do you get the arousal and how does it get calmed down, the perceptual and motor systems we need to run through these. You can look at Dan Siegel's work.

For a lot of these, the two hemispheres of the brain, people say, well, we do the bilateral stimulation, and that's what makes the EMDR effect, because it's the two hemispheres of the brain ... that's one of the theories, and then other people say, well, it's the triune brain actually, because it's the neocortex and it's the limbic system and it's the brainstem.

Well, yeah, because you have this and you have this. In other words, there's so many relevant systems involved, and there are theories about EMDR in terms of its procedures and the stimulation that are linked into all of these, and the bottom line is we still don't know, but these are all of the ones that have been implicated and the individual parts of the brain. Because when you do the eye movement, you get the PGO spikes, which also stimulate the hippocampus, and that's the memory center, and then of course the corpus callosum is also involved. And it's the neoelectrical system because it's the linkages that are going on in terms of the electrical stimulation.

Fidelity of the model

But then you also have the endocrine system that's going on, and so if you take all of this, we're basically going, what's involved in processing? I'd say it's that and it's not that. It's not that I say that neurobiology is not important. Of course it is. It's the basis of everything, but we don't know, nor do we need to know at this time, what the biological underpinnings are. We're going by what we're seeing clinically, and so fidelity does count. I heard somebody say fidelity only counts in research. No, fidelity counts all the time.

And I'm taking the feedback from clinicians that have worked with the EMDR since 1990. One in particular is working, talking to me recently—she's been working with combat veterans for a long time and over the years. She felt she was doing really good work, and then she decided to do a research project and had to put the fidelity checklist in there, so she had to do it exactly according to protocol, and she realized how much better results she was getting than she had gotten before because of the drift. Because we let go of things that aren't quite comfortable, and we bring in things that are more comfortable.

But the bottom line is that if you eliminate aspects of the procedures that have been tested, you might be leaving out the relevant brain functions that are necessary to give the most effective and efficient results, and that's the only reason that we're saying do it as it's been researched and as it's been standardized, because this is what we know work[s].

Flow, attunement and therapists' fear

So let's go to another problem. We are dealing with a dyad. One of the things that we are hoping to have clinicians being more aware of is their impact on the client. Can I as a clinician, one, can I as a clinician support my client? Can I unite with the client? Am I feeling present and whole? Can I link with the client into one attuned unit? Can I maintain a value of compassion? If not, what techniques do I have to employ on me, because if I'm feeling anxious or worrying about the mortgage or looking at the ceiling, it's there. The client gets it. And how do I make a decision about when they're going too far into the experience and I'm losing them, or when I have to use an interweave, and also am I knowledgeable about this population I'm working with? Because I know EMDR does not mean I should be working with a substance abuse client, because I don't know the issues involved in the substance abuse client.

So I have consultation. Same thing with DID, same thing with any of the specialties, so this, you know, I've heard them say, folks say, well, EMDR, the relationship isn't important. Yes, the relationship is important. You are the pillar. You're the linkage. You are the one that put this golden protective bubble around the two of you so that you can connect.

Clinicians' fear impedes the process

It's very important who you are and what do you need to do to feel present and not afraid of what the person is going to be experiencing. Are you all right with what they need to experience, or are you going to say to them, "No, you don't have to feel that right now; no, it's okay"? Just think, everyone has different tolerance levels, affect tolerance levels. What's yours?

If you see a client feeling their disturbance, do you have the sense it's dangerous for them? Are you telling your client, "Don't feel; be afraid of your feelings"? Are you giving them the same messages that they got early on: "Don't feel it. Don't express it. The other person will run away. The other person will think it's shameful. I'll disintegrate." All those messages that are in there. Have you cleaned them out of your system? Because processing means the client will go where they need to go, and are you ready to let them do that? There's the dual awareness for them of one foot in the past and one foot in the present, noticing it as it emerges.

This is where the preparation phase comes in. What do you have to teach them so you know they can stay present with you? Can both people in our dyad allow the information to flow and let whatever happens happen? Are you willing to do it? Can they do it?

We don't want them to be afraid of the fear! If not, what do I have to teach so that they can let go of disturbance? What techniques? Preparation is just, can the client close down the disturbance in the session, and do they have something to allow them to close down the disturbance between sessions? If they can do that, you can process. You simply don't want them to be afraid of it, and you want to make sure they can stay present with you. Most clients need very little preparation because they are primarily intact. The long preparation phases are for the more fragmented, dissociated, unstable because they have a tendency to be more afraid of their body, their fear not to be associated. But long preparation is not for everyone. It's for those who need it. Can I maintain the same focus and use interweaves again? What do I do to mimic spontaneous processing and get out of the way to alter stimuli—eye movement, taps, tones—and for me to stay present?

You do not need excessive resourcing; find one that works

It's for those who need it. Can I maintain the same focus and use interweaves? Again, what do I do to mimic spontaneous processing and get out of the way, to alter stimuli, eye movement, taps, tones, and for me to stay present? It's to close down disturbance. And all of these different stress reduction —there's been so many names for them over the years, stress reduction techniques, self-control techniques, now they'll be calling affect regulation techniques, whatever you call them, making sure that there's an availability of positive networks.

That's all it means. They can get to the positive network when we need it to let whatever happens, happen, and to close down the system. Do I teach mindfulness, guided imagery, hypnosis, the light stream technique, putting the disturbance into a container, ways of grounding? Do I do what's called ego state work, using a healing circle to prepare them? Do I do inner child work? Do I do a safe place? Or do I need a calm place or a centered place or an empowered place? That's what they need to stay present and to close down the disturbance.

Do I do resource development, imaginal work, somatic work, breathing work? Use it all. Have it all. Have it all.

But you don't have to teach your clients all of these. Find one that works for them. It's great to have all the arrows.

You don't have to teach them all of this. You just have to have it so that they can let whatever happens happen in the session and you can close down disturbance. Does it make sense? Okay.

Three-pronged approach and second order conditioning

Three-pronged protocol. Three. So it's one, me as a therapist.

Two, the dual awareness. Three, pronged protocol. What are the targets for processing?

Past: What memories set the foundation? Two, present: What situations trigger the disturbance? What does that mean? What upset you last week? That's a present situation. What places do they go? What things do they do that bring up disturbance? We need to process that.

Why? Because the earlier events that have been set in motion are the stored experiences that have to be processed through. But what is disturbing them in the present may also be the result of second-order conditioning, meaning if I'm disturbed and I walk into this room a hundred times when I'm disturbed, then these different stimuli in these rooms have gotten conditioned to cause me disturbance. So even if I process the earlier stuff, this is now independent.

Behavioral psychology. Process the present. And you're getting a log and feedback.

What's still disturbing? What's still disturbing? A lot of stuff will have dropped away. And future. For each characteristic, for each dysfunction, future template.

Why? We're preparing the client with the skills and behaviors and information necessary for optimal functioning in the future. The multiply molested clients or multiply abused clients or neglected clients, developmentally deficient clients need to have those experiences engendered by you in your office that lets them know if they yell at you, that you're still going to be there, you're not going to run away, and if you get disturbed at them, you're going to still be there, you're not going to run away. And they can feel connection.

Future template

All of these things that they should have learned in childhood that they didn't learn in childhood, you have to bring in. And so the experiential templates for the future templates involve bringing in through the experience with you, our imaginable, new things that they need, having them feel it in their body and processing it if there's a negative cognition of "I can't do it," the positive cognition, the whole protocol. As they're feeling it and then have them imagine doing it.

And then after you've had them imagine doing it, you've set a template. What does that mean? A connection of networks that when they go out, this is most likely what's going to light up, and then they'll do the behaviors and they'll get the feedback in the real world, and hopefully it will be reinforced. And if it's not, they write it down in a log and you know what else you need to process.

So it's a feedback loop. So I want to get a show of hands, please. Well, everything I've said so far, the gestalt event, for how many of you is this clear? Oh, thank God.

Okay. Because this is going to let you judge everything that comes along, everything that people suggest. Does it fit in here? Okay.

Start with the past. When's the first time you remember it? Again, because of the possibility of the feeder memories, and it was the foundation. Four aspects of memory.

In other words, in that protocol, how do I line it up? How do I get to it? The primary manifestations are the image, the cognition, the belief the person has, the emotion, which is just kind of sad. Didn't really do it, you know? The emotion's like the colors—red, green, blue, or the rainbow. That whole light spring.

When I say I'm sad, it's my color. There's no images. And as we access it, all the sense experiences are involved.

If they say, well, I'm smelling something, you don't say, well, ignore that. Just go to the image over there. It's whatever it is that comes up.

Positive outcomes are relevant to positive alignment. Image, negative thought, emotion, physical sensation. Why do we use the positive cognition? We're lighting up the positive networks, giving them a guidance and lighting up the network so it makes it easier to link in.

Manifestations of memory. Just think of it. I'm going to run through this pretty quickly.

But in ways of getting negative and positive cognitions, in your manuals, you've got the list of different cognitions. You can hand it to the client. Young Schema Therapy has ... What? I said I'd go over it.

Yeah. Young has different possible schema. It doesn't mean that one client's going to have them all.

It gets you sensitized to be able to hear it. Okay. Okay.

Going back to this, five is this, because this is major. Five fingers and channels. Have I allowed the processing to progress? Have I let them be accessed and processed without distortion? Have I checked my work? Remember? Have I gone back undistorted? And the outside reach, meaning, am I getting feedback from when they go back into their world? How has it been within session, between sessions, and the following session, in other words, and at termination.

Comprehensive use of EMDR and warning to therapists

You should be going through all of the major memories. You should be dealing with their relationships, with all their significant others at that point. What comes up for them? You don't want to let the client out.

Well, you know, it's like not asked or anything, but you don't ... The notion is you want to do comprehensive therapy. So if they're there, give it the best shot. Because the issue is we want the clients to come out with a sense of ... a positive sense.

But what are you looking at here? We have ... Life is a rose. You start them doing processing with something, and then as they're going through it, you get kind of afraid of their affect a little bit, and you trigger a resource, and you go into this sense of, yeah, life is good, and I'm feeling great, you know. But, you know, if you look a little closer, you see what's going on here. There's real intimacy involved here.

But you didn't let them go where they needed to go, and where they needed to go was to go through a fear of death. You didn't let them get there. So you were being nice.

You wanted them to feel better. You thought you had the answer, and you put a Band-Aid across some channel that they never got to. Let them go where they need to go, because who knows what memories lurk.

Allow the clients their own associations to progress unimpeded. Okay. You'll have the quick list.

So EMDR. There's a difference between desensitization and reprocessing. Folks that I've seen who call it desensitize the trauma are missing—there's a misunderstanding here.

Desensitization you can get with lots and lots of different types of therapies and techniques. It simply means you got down from a ten to a zero, and there's lots of ways to do that. This is processing.

Learning has taken place. Emotional, cognitive, changes in body. This is what we're looking for.

In EMDR, desensitization is only one byproduct of the reprocessing. If you're not seeing cognitive shifts, if you're not seeing differences in posture, if you're not seeing new sense of self, think about whether you're really doing the processing or whether you're just doing resource and desensitization. This is part of the, and that's why support groups are good, and that's why getting other consensus reality issues are good here.

You see this? Which table is bigger? Longer? Wider? Wrong. They're exactly the same. When you leave, you're going to get a handout, and you're going to have that on it.

Take a look. Because whatever the perceptual cues are, one, they're exactly the same. We have certain things that we bring to the party that are going to cause us to see certain things.

We have to make sure that there's an analysis, like put your finger on it, on your handout, and see whether it's the same as one or the other. Because for all of us at EMDR, I really want to honor all clinicians and innovators for wanting to bring stuff to the party. Please, I've gotten folks who have told me, well, we don't use the cognitions because according to Dan Siegel's work, children's brains develop at a different rate, and if it's younger than a certain, you shouldn't use cognitions.

And so I took what they said, and I sent it to Dan Siegel, and he said, well, tell me what you think. And he said, that's not the way the brain works. So there was a misunderstanding.

So if you're going to be suggesting protocols on the basis of neurobiology, please make sure that you've had a consultation with the expert in the field to check your assumptions. Of course, we've already had a couple of instances where it just isn't true. The other is, if you're changing protocols, what's your data? Because what Amen's results were, what the research results were, were based on standard protocols.

Don't change the protocol

If you're changing your protocol, and it feels good in your office, take the time to get the data. Because, as Rosalie mentioned, ethically, according to APA, EMDR, as it is with any other form of therapy, are the tested standard protocols. If they're not doing the protocols, so just be clear.

All we're talking about is clarity. And the bottom line is, more clinical ways of doing the history-taking, fabulous. More ways of doing preparation, great.

More ways of evaluating, terrific. But this ends up ... You'll have these in your handouts. Am I getting ... Yeah, okay. Altering the standard protocol—NO!!!!!

Responsibility. I want you to have the sense here is, and there's a really good poster, so I won't go into this talking, but when your client is saying, "I'm damaged because of a rape," just as in many cultures in Bangladesh, the acid victims who were shamed because of it, and they took on a sense of, there's something wrong with me, it's because of what the society accepted, societal mores. This, too, can be processed.

I think there's a really good poster that would talk about it there. So areas of confusion, please, are the difference between mechanism, model, and methodology. The neurobiology, it doesn't matter which are the mechanisms, it's still the model, guiding principles.

The methodology are the procedures and protocols. There's a difference between technique and approach. If all you do is pull out EMDR to do it when someone's, quote, stuck, you're doing a technique.

If you're viewing it as the information and what do I look for in case conceptualization, this is EMDR as an approach. Now, the difference between symptom reduction and comprehensive treatment, the difference between accessing and processing—just because you brought it up doesn't mean it's processing. You need to see the movement through the channels.

Adequate preparation described and the difference between necessary and adequate resources

The client has adequate resources to process if they can close down disturbance and let whatever happens, happen. You don't have to give them every resource they need for an entire life before you start processing.

And the ability to recognize negative and positive experiential contributors. Because information processing involves many things. It'll be in your handout.

I'm going to move through this. But this is the bottom line. What are you concentrating on? What am I focused on? Symptom reduction? Am I stuck with this?

The client came in with a phobia. The client came in because this is a complaint. Is this all I'm going to do? Or do I look at the entire picture? Because processing involves all of this. And the client won't even know it's possible unless you let them know.

So thanks for staying for these extra few minutes. No question. Thank you.

Appendix Three

The Language of the Unconscious

As I said, these phrases are common, overused, but highly generalizable through a client's life. These open channels to process that are often ignored.

I don't want to be around you.
I don't like uninvited touching.
I'm always walking on thin ice.
There is nothing in the box, but it's not empty.
I never got a break.
I got to get out of here.
I better not push it.
Why do I only love people who hate me?
If it stops, I'm in danger.
I can't breathe.
I need to get out of here.
It came out of the blue.
I'm going to die in here.
I'm like a chicken running around without a head.

Once you lose everything, there is nothing more to fear.
What just happened?
I have to fix it.
I still don't know.
What am I going to do?
Here we go again.
Hanging on for dear life.
Going off by myself made things easier.
My best isn't good enough.
I played to their tune not to mine.
A horse is only as good as its rider.
I should have spent more time with him.
I feel out of sorts.
I'm a living monument to my mother's sins.
I was the light in their life.
They're messing with my plans.
It's hard to swallow.
I can't see what's up ahead.
I'm a lesser class of being.
Why does everyone take what's mine?
Trying to take a feather out of my cap.
I'm ready to get down in the dirt.
Happily married all by myself.
I see a field of pink petunias.
Can't please 'em.

Acknowledgments

I want to thank my wife, JoAnne, who understands me better than anyone on the planet. She has been my partner for almost fifty years. She motivates me to want to be the best version of myself that I can be. She has always supported my life, as I have tried to support hers. I think J.D. Salinger described the relationship I have with my wife perfectly when he wrote: "She wasn't doing much of anything as best I could tell, just leaning on the second-floor balcony railing and holding my universe together."

Second, I want to thank Theresa Wunderlich, my executive assistant, who organizes my life in ways that are beyond my ability. I could not do any of the things I do without her endless caring, devotion, and support. People who know me professionally know Theresa, and they often say, "I need to find an assistant like her." I reply, there is no one like her. I thank God every day for bringing her skill and expertise into my world.

I also want to thank Chris Kridler, who came into my life when a random Uber driver took me to the airport and sold me a book he had just written. He could not stop heaping praise on his editor, Chris Kridler. I was finishing my first book and needed an editor. That is what Robert A. Johnson would call a slender thread. A seemingly random encounter that changed my life. That was over ten years ago. To call Chris an editor hardly covers all that she does. I am sure my books would never have seen the light of day without her patience, skill, and experience supporting my projects.

I also want to thank Elisa Planellas, my social media expert. After all these years of working with me, doing her own EMDR work, and reading everything I ever wrote about EMDR, when she writes content on my behalf, what she writes sounds like me. Her niche is EMDR. And she is highly skilled in what she does for me and other EMDR therapists. I am very grateful for her skill and commitment to our work and to EMDR.

I want to thank all of my co-authors. Without them, I doubt this book would have been written. This book was born out of my work as a consultant to my co-authors. It was these therapists' fascination with my work and my approach that started the formal development of Transformation EMDR. They started saying things like, I had a transformational EMDR session today. I knew what they were talking about; I just never put it into those words. Each of these six other contributors was instrumental in highlighting the need for this book.

Ryan Terry, I believe, was the first one to coin the term Transformational EMDR. Elena Engle has been an EMDR therapist the longest. I trained her when I first started training EMDR therapists over six years ago. She was pregnant with her son, Charlie, at the time. I recall that during one of our initial training calls, she was working at the school and they had an active shooter drill. She asked me to hold on because she had to get under her desk. I responded, "How are you going to do that? You're about ready to have a baby." Somehow, she got under the desk, and we continued. She took some time off to care for her son, along with her husband, Rob, who became interested in EMDR shortly after Elena began her certification. Rob, also a certified EMDR therapist, has an interest in dreams and Jung. He was a perfect fit for our team. These three clinicians keep me young and excited about the work. I am truly gratified to have such great people in my professional and personal world.

Melinda Johnson and Linda Khmelnytska started their EMDR journey with Ryan at the same training back in 2021. They all attended the same initial fifty-hour EMDR training, which took place almost five years ago. Melinda brings a varied world of life experiences. She is a military veteran, worked in law enforcement, and became a social worker about a dozen years ago. She, too, began to separate EMDR sessions from Transformational EMDR sessions early on. She has also written a book about Eastern Orthodox religion and EMDR; keep an eye out for her book.

Linda Khmelnytska is Ukrainian American and became sold on EMDR in that very first EMDR training. I think she told me at that training that I don't charge enough for "this incredible training," which, I believe, was her exact quote. It was clear she was amazed and excited at the power of EMDR and worked very hard to become an extraordinary T-EMDR therapist, which she is.

Dunja Pacirski is another international therapist. I actually met Dunja before I began training EMDR therapists myself. I was assisting another trainer when I met Dunja. She did all of her subsequent EMDR consultations with me after our initial meeting, and our professional relationship has continued over the years. She has been excited about EMDR since that day. Her calm and friendly demeanor makes her easily accessible to both consultants and patients. Her world experiences in the US and in Croatia make her an invaluable part of my team.

Carolyn Lenz attended my basic training and continued her training through the EMDRIA certification process with me. She was not planning to become an approved consultant. I, however, insisted that she reconsider, because she is a natural leader and teacher, and she excels at EMDR. I am glad she did. She is an excellent asset to my team, her consultees, and her patients. Her experience as a therapist, combined with her own EMDR journey, makes her an invaluable asset.

These T-EMDR therapists consistently inspire me with their enthusiasm for this work every day. I am so appreciative of their dedication when they assist me in my training. They are dedicated to those who come to me for training as much as they are committed to their patients.

From the bottom of my heart, I want to thank these six clinicians who fulfilled the promise that Jung talked about. "If you do good, conscientious work, unknown allies will come and seek you out," as I said at the beginning of this book and reiterated here. He was absolutely right.

Finally, I want to thank Francine Shapiro, who left us an enormous amount of literature, and for that 2003 keynote address that is the cornerstone of this book and for the incredible discovery that is EMDR.

ALSO BY DR. ANDREW J. DOBO

Unburdening Souls at the Speed of Thought: Psychology, Christianity, and the Transforming Power of EMDR

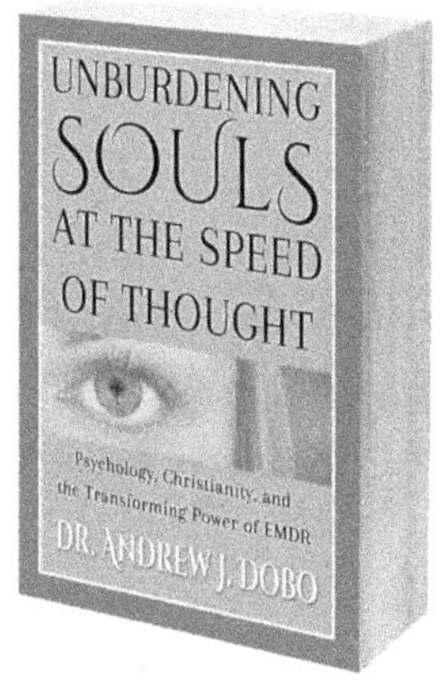

Unburdening Souls at the Speed of Thought: Psychology, Christianity, and the Transforming Power of EMDR is about the transformative journey to wholeness that was modeled by Christ and is accelerated by a groundbreaking therapy known as EMDR (Eye Movement Desensitization and Reprocessing).

You will see an emotionally scarred surfer recover from the ultimate loss, the tragic death of his son. You will learn how dreams and images gave subjects the courage to change careers and enrich their lives. And you will discover how a woman accessed a buried traumatic memory during a therapy session and gained an enduring sense of peace.

The process described in psychologist Dr. Andrew J. Dobo's book occurs in six stages, which are mirrored by six moments Christ modeled in his Passion. Psychology and religion collide in the book's incredible tales, which move from despair to hope, hate to love, and fear to contentment.

This is a book that will give hope to those suffering

mental anguish as they are exposed to a new map of the soul modeled by Christ and shared by psychology. It shows how survivors of trauma can heal and overcome negative beliefs about themselves. It's for those who want to better understand the workings of the soul and for those who do not even imagine such a thing exists. And it will fascinate any reader interested in the power of the mind.

The Hero's Journey: Integrating Jungian Psychology and EMDR Therapy

A new language of healing for EMDR

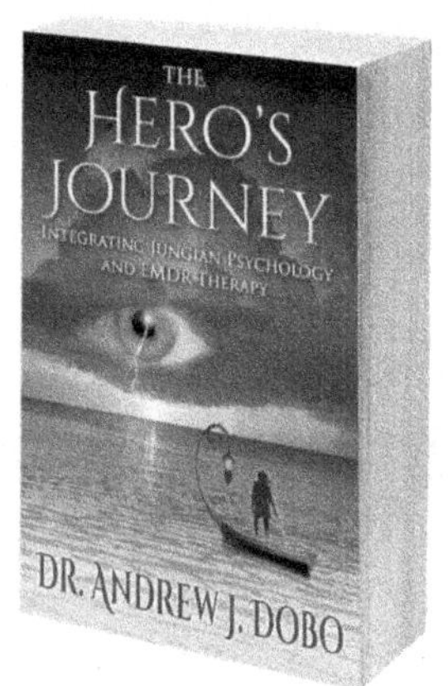

The hero's journey made famous by Joseph Campbell and seen in countless iconic stories also offers a therapeutic map for healing, as psychologist and teacher Dr. Andrew J. Dobo reveals in *The Hero's Journey: Integrating Jungian Psychology and EMDR Therapy*.

EMDR therapy, which uses bilateral stimulation to help clients process traumatic and troubling pasts, helps them live out their own hero's journey and find their path to a new way of life. Dr. Dobo's book shows how the stages of the hero's journey offer a powerful parallel to the stages of healing in EMDR.

Through the lens of Jungian psychology, Dr. Dobo unveils how therapists can be companions on this hero's journey by watching for crucial clues and gently guiding clients to healing. He shows how recognizing seemingly insignificant statements during sessions can unveil stunning truths about clients' lives that will help them move past their pain and into the realm of hope.

In his knowledgeable, accessible style, Dr. Dobo demonstrates that by combining creativity, a new understanding of the language of the unconscious in the context of mythology, and Francine Shapiro's standard EMDR protocol, therapists can learn to magnify their healing skills while discovering their own inner genius.

Contributors

Ryan Terry, LMHC

Ryan Terry is a Licensed Mental Health Counselor, Certified EMDR Therapist, an EMDRIA Approved Consultant and Trainer in training. He is the founder of Sunrise EMDR, a holistic practice in Jacksonville Beach, Florida, specializing in individual therapy EMDR intensives, group retreats, and movement-based therapies set along the First Coast beaches.

Ryan's approach integrates mindfulness, Jungian psychology, ancient stories, addiction recovery, attachment work, dream exploration, and movement therapies, with a lifelong core interest in the intersecting space between science and the sacred, to create opportunities for deep self-healing transformation to occur.

We are entering a new era of EMDR and mental

health treatment, one that honors both the scientific and the sacred dimensions of healing. Many of us today hunger for something deeper than symptom relief. We seek meaning, wholeness, and transformation.

This book stands as a guide for that evolution. It provides EMDR therapists with a thoughtful framework for integrating the sacred into their work, helping clients awaken to the deeper purpose within their pain and become who they were always meant to be.

Dr. Dobo has illuminated this path with clarity and compassion. As those who have not forgotten the transformative power of crisis can offer, in the same spirit of what the Japanese kanji for "crisis" reminds us: Danger is followed by opportunity. This book embodies that truth.

I am honored to endorse this work and invite every reader to enter their own process of growth, learning and unlearning, as we continue the sacred task of accompanying individuals toward a deeper healing, and thus the world to a deeper peace.

Elena Engle, LMHC-S

Elena Engle, LMHC-S, is a Certified EMDR Therapist and EMDRIA Approved Consultant. She emphasizes ethical, attuned and transformational EMDR practice that help clients and clinicians move from survival to sustainable, values-aligned living. She co-leads a hybrid EMDR private practice serving Florida and North Carolina and facilitates EMDR consultation groups that respects the nervous system, honors client autonomy, and invites genuine change rather than quick fixes.

> *I'm grateful to contribute to a volume that elevates both the science and the soul of our field. This is a book to study, teach from, and return to whenever you need clarity and courage in the therapy room.*

Carolyn Lenz, LMHC

Carolyn Lenz, LMHC, is an EMDRIA Certified Therapist, EMDR Consultant, and Transformational EMDR™ Certified Practitioner with a multi-state private practice based in Tampa Bay, Florida. Carolyn was first introduced to EMDR through her own mental health journey, where she experienced the profound healing and personal growth brought forth by EMDR therapy. The experience of working with a skilled and supportive EMDR therapist planted the seeds of change.

With over a decade of experience supporting trauma survivors and mentoring clinicians, Carolyn's passion lies in guiding others toward living authentically and lasting personal growth. When she discovered Dr. Dobo's approach to Transformational EMDR™, she recognized the powerful return to Dr. Shapiro's original vision—healing that extends beyond symptom relief into true integration and growth. Honored to join the co-author team for this work, Carolyn believes Transformational EMDR™ has the potential to inspire clinicians to facilitate change that transforms both their clients—and themselves.

M.H. Johnson, LCSW

M.H. Johnson, LCSW, is an EMDRIA Certified Therapist and Approved Consultant in private practice. She works, writes, speaks, and lives at the intersection of mental and spiritual health. Melinda was initially drawn to EMDR for its evidence-based application for healing trauma, but when she encountered Dr. Dobo's Transformational EMDR, she realized the transformational shift that extends deeper than commonly practiced.

Her message to other therapists interested in deep healing is simple: Once you experience Transformational EMDR, you won't go back, and neither will your clients. A military veteran, Melinda received her undergraduate degree in economics from Georgetown University and her Master of Social Work from Florida State University. She lives with her family in Jensen Beach, Florida.

Dr. Dunja Pačirski, LCSW

Dr. Dunja Pačirski, LCSW, EMDR Approved Consultant and T-EMDR Trainer in Training, is dedicated to helping individuals transform the impact of trauma into pathways of mental and emotional resilience. With over two decades of clinical experience, she guides her private practice with a personal and professional vision: helping people find inner peace and expand in joy for Self, Life, and each other.

After she crossed paths with Dr. Andrew Dobo, EMDR became more than a therapeutic method for her—it evolved into an art of healing. Following years of clinical work in the United States and the completion of her doctoral studies at Barry University in Miami, Dr. Pačirski returned to her hometown of Zagreb, Croatia, to found New Beginnings: Center for Emotional Wellness—a sanctuary for those seeking to rewrite the emotional imprints of trauma and reclaim the parts of themselves lost to pain. Her work reminds us that healing is not about forgetting; it is about transforming.

By passing forward the education and mentorship she received from Dr. Dobo in Transformational EMDR, she is cultivating a new generation of trauma-informed clinicians equipped to use EMDR with mindful presence, confidence, and compassion. Through T-EMDR, she invites both clients and clinicians to recognize that transformation is not only possible, but a truth already waiting within—and every ending can mark a new beginning.

Linda Khmelnytska, LMHC

Linda Khmelnytska, LMHC, is an EMDRIA Certified Therapist and Approved Consultant in private practice in Tampa

Bay, Florida. Linda was drawn to EMDR after finding that traditional therapeutic models failed to create the depth of change her clients needed. EMDR became the bridge between insight and transformation—a method that consistently delivered what others promised but rarely achieved. Linda utilizes EMDR not only in her clinical practice but also internationally, providing group EMDR for trauma recovery and disaster-relief efforts.

Trained in Ukraine and licensed in the United States, Linda brings a global and integrative perspective to her EMDR work. She is dedicated to preserving the integrity of Shapiro's original model while embracing the deeper healing potential revealed through Dr. Andrew Dobo's Transformational EMDR approach.

Linda was honored to contribute to this book, which she believes captures the essence of Transformational EMDR, where structure meets intuition and therapy becomes a vehicle for profound human change.

Robert Engle, LMHC

Robert Engle, LMHC, is a trauma and neurodiversity specialist and a Certified EMDR therapist. He blends transformational EMDR with performance psychology and practical systems thinking. He co-leads a hybrid EMDR private practice serving Florida and North Carolina and is a business coach for therapists from integrating EMDR's Eight Phases and the AIP Model into running a business.

I'm certain that any EMDR therapist can enhance

their skills and expand the clinical framework to truly be transformational with this book. I know this is a rare guide you can return to because of the trustworthy roadmap it unfolds of both science and the soul. I'm grateful to be at a seat at the table with Dr. Dobo and these accomplished colleagues.

About the Author

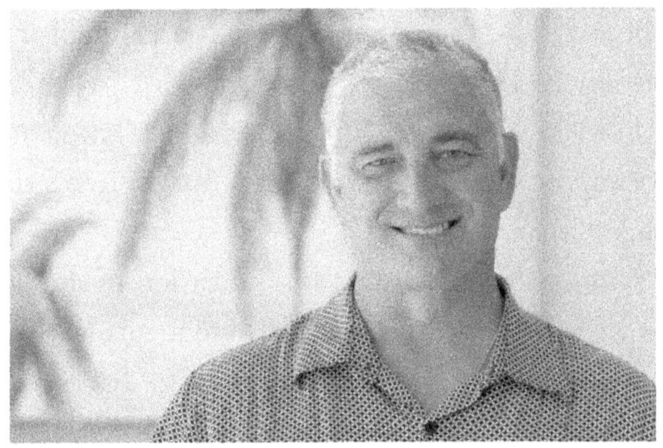

Dr. Andrew J. Dobo was first trained in EMDR in 1998 while in graduate school. He has administered over 15,000 EMDR sessions in his career. Now his days are spent consulting, writing, and teaching other therapists about EMDR therapy.

Dr. Dobo is highly credentialed in EMDR and has lived his life as a Jungian. He recorded his first dream in 1978 while studying music as a young man living in Chicago. He has never stopped using his dreams as navigational tools in his life. He eventually noticed that as he was using the EMDR model, he was also integrating Jungian thought, which included dreams to explain the EMDR process with his clients. This observation eventually gave rise to his books.

It became clear to him that EMDR activated a transformation journey that the clients were invited to travel during his work with them. He noticed the clients moved through six stages and these six stages encompassed the twelve steps of a hero's journey identified by Joseph Campbell.

These observations were the catalyst for this book and his innovative EMDR trainings.

He hopes more therapists will see the value of myth that exists during EMDR. He invites every EMDR therapist to try and hold mythic space in our evidence-based model of EMDR therapy, because there is room for both to exist in the same space simultaneously.

His previous work led to a formalization of the Transformational EMDR approach, which is what this book is about. Transformational EMDR goes beyond the disease model of EMDR therapy, which was an aspiration of Francine Shapiro's when she said, "[Self]-actualization for everyone." Shapiro never specifically explained how one might use EMDR in this manner, but this book explains precisely how to transform a client's life in a way that gets them to change course and move in the direction of their authentic life's purpose. It is a guide toward self-actualization and individuation.

You can connect with Dr. Dobo on social media.

Website: EMDReducators.com

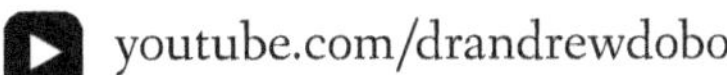
youtube.com/drandrewdobo

facebook.com/emdreducators

linkedin.com/in/dr-andrew-j-dobo-36595673

instagram.com/emdr_educators

www.ingramcontent.com/pod-product-compliance
Lightning Source LLC
Chambersburg PA
CBHW031117020426
42333CB00012B/124

* 9 7 8 0 9 9 6 2 2 0 7 8 1 *